Endorsements for R_

"These delightful stories will warm your heart and teach you powerful lessons about love and grace."
—Jack Canfield, cocreator of
Chicken Soup for the Soul

"With a Max Lucado writing style, Chris Karcher shares powerful insights through stories of encouragement and hope."
—Lea Ann Lobb, KUTV, Salt Lake City, Utah
Television News Anchor

" 'Grace,' writes Philip Yancey, 'is the last best word of the church.' Many books have been written about grace, fewer perhaps have been written with it. This one is grace-full."
—John Ortberg, author of
Everybody's Normal Till You Get To Know Them

"Chris Karcher provides readers with ageless and universal spiritual truths and speaks relevantly and eloquently to modern souls traveling through this century of uncertainty. For all those living in the world, but not of it, she lights the path for the burdened and challenges the enlightened. Each page is overflowing with grace and relevant blessings for those wise enough to partake. No matter what stage or situation of life it is your gift to occupy, you will find it easier to awaken to grace."
—Foster Cline, M.D., cofounder with Jim Fay of the
Love and Logic philosophy

"This is a warm, wonderful, inspiring book full of timeless truths and wisdom to make you feel good about yourself."
—Brian Tracy, author of
Create Your Own Future

"Inner peace, grace-filled living, an overwhelming sense of being loved . . . You will discover these life-changing realities and much more as you immerse yourself in *Relationships of Grace*. Chris Karcher's style is incredible—great stories and illustrations, powerful truths, and a gripping intensity."
—Glenna Salsbury, CSP, CPAE Speaker Hall of Fame
Past President National Speakers Association
Author of *The Art of the Fresh Start*

"In *Relationships of Grace,* Christine Karcher inspires us to create loving relationships with God, others, and ourselves. By sharing stories from scripture and everyday life, she reminds us that we have not only the choice, but the responsibility to accept and love ourselves, others, and God. Christine fills us with the joyful realization that, by the grace of God, we can live as the person He created us to be!"
—LeAnn Thieman, coauthor of
Chicken Soup for the Christian Woman's Soul
and *Chicken Soup for the Nurse's Soul*

"Many 'relationship' books pay lip service to the spiritual dimension of relationships. We should all thank Chris Karcher for putting spirituality front-and-center in *Relationships of Grace*."
—Gregory J.P. Godek, author of
1001 Ways to be Romantic

"Embracing and appropriating God's grace empowers us to live that grace in relationships with others. Chris has done a magnificent job of revealing the challenge, example, and process of 'grace living.' "
—Naomi Rhode, CSP, CPAE Speaker Hall of Fame
Past President National Speakers Association

Relationships
of
Grace

Resources by Chris Karcher

Amazing Things I Know About You
Relationships of Grace Workbook
Relationships of Grace
Relationships of Grace CD
Relationships of Grace audiocassette

Relationships
of Grace

*Spiritual keys for
creating loving relationships,
loving yourself, and
living with meaning*

CHRIS KARCHER

 AdamsKing Publishing

Published by AdamsKing Publishing
AdamsKing Publishing, P.O. Box 1043, Layton, Utah 84041-1043
Email: info@adamsking.com

Cover design by George Foster, www.fostercovers.com.

Publisher's Cataloging-in-Publication Data

Karcher, Chris.
    Relationships of grace : spiritual keys for creating loving relationships, loving yourself, and living with meaning / Chris Karcher.
    p. cm.
    Includes bibliographical references.
    LCCN 2003101085
    ISBN 1-932356-51-7

    1. Spiritual life. 2. Interpersonal relations—Religious aspects. 3. God—Knowableness. 4. Self-esteem—Religious aspects. 5. Grace (Theology) 6. Love—Religious aspects. I. Title.

BL626.33.K37 2003   291.4'4

10 9 8 7 6 5 4 3 2 1
First Edition

To four incredible gifts of grace:

My husband, Dave

My daughter, Erin

and

My parents, William C. and Beverly S. Nester

Share Your Story

We welcome your stories, thoughts, and insight. Please feel free to provide feedback and share how your life has been impacted by *Relationships of Grace.*

You are also invited to submit a story, anecdote, or quotation for possible inclusion in our next book, *Relationships of Grace Miracles.* This may be your own original material or something you have read that was written by someone else. Both the author and contributor will be acknowledged. A seventy-five-word biography of the author will be included. Multiple submissions are welcome. For additional information, please see the page at the back of this book entitled "Share Your Story in Our Next Book *Relationships of Grace Miracles*" or visit www.RelationshipsOfGrace.com.

Please share your experiences, stories, and reactions to *Relationships of Grace* by sending them to:

feedback@RelationshipsOfGrace.com
www.RelationshipsOfGrace.com

Relationships of Grace
P.O. Box 1043
Layton, Utah 84041-1043
Fax: 801-547-0928

Contents

Acknowledgments

To my editor, Chandra Sparks Taylor: Your red pen flows with skill; your heart flows with kindness.

To the wonderful people who reviewed portions of the manuscript: Pat Alexander, Lea Ann Asbury, Kathy Drabek, Erin Karcher, Myra Martin, Georgette Rowe, Tammy Stevenson, and my anonymous friend. You challenged me with your insight and thought-provoking comments. I am grateful for your review and even more grateful for your friendship.

To my dear friend Florence Beal: Thank you for all you have taught me through your own personal example.

To my anonymous friend: I am blessed to have you as a mentor and friend. Your wisdom is woven into the words of this book.

To the following extraordinary people who have graced my life: Vickie, Dennis, Jason, Laurie, Matthew, Campy, Quentin, Maryann, Alex, Brandon, Andrew, Richard, Marilyn, Julie, Dick, Ricky, Courtney, Ted, Jean, Savanna, and Risa. You have all contributed in your own way to the tapestry that follows.

To my mom and dad, Beverly and William Nester: Thank you for all the lessons, laughter, and love. I will never be able to repay you for all you have done for me—as it always is with grace, the math is too outrageous.

To my husband, Dave, and my daughter, Erin: After endless hours of penning a plethora of words, I find myself at an uncharacteristic loss of them—because there are no words to express what you mean to me. I cannot imagine my life without you.

And to you, the reader: I am honored you have chosen to read this book. I hope you are abundantly blessed with relationships of grace.

CHAPTER ONE

Moonbeams of Grace

Eight children buzzed with excitement at the starting line for a Special Olympics race. Glowing in anticipation, they searched the crowd for familiar faces. Shoes tied and spirits high, they took their places.

"On your mark, get set, go," the starter signaled. They were off. The children began as a pack. Before long, the fastest runners forged ahead.

One of the slower boys tripped and scraped his knee as he tumbled to the ground. With a quivering lip and troubled heart, tears rolled down his cheeks.

A girl with Down syndrome heard her opponent's whimper and watched as he wiped his eyes. Although she was well on her way to victory, she stopped and ran back to help her fallen friend. The girl administered the only treatment needed: This runner-turned-nurse kneeled, kissed her friend's knee better, and patted away his tears.

Before long, all of the other racers turned back to comfort their friend and help him up. With all the racers on their feet again, they all set off to finish the race. As the children approached the finish line, it was a sight to behold. A sea of smiles silhouetted the sidelines. Eyes were moist with tears. Hearts overflowed in wonder. Triumph filled the air.

Down the final stretch they came. All eight racers walked toward the finish line with their arms linked. They held their heads high in sheer delight.

The racers cheered and the crowd roared as all eight children crossed the finish line together—arm in arm.

Yearning for Love

Isn't that what we all want—to make the journey through life linked arm in arm with the people we care about?

As different as people appear on the surface, deep inside, we are the same. We hunger for love. We long for a full life and to connect with others. Meaning enters our lives through our relationships with God, others, and self.

We were created to experience love through deep, meaningful relationships. All of the Ten Commandments are decrees about relationships. Five words summarize Jesus' teachings about all the laws in the Bible: "Love God, neighbor, and self."[1] The book of Romans explains, "Love satisfies all of God's requirements."[2] John the Disciple wrote, "Love one another, for love comes from God. Everyone who loves has been born of God and knows God."[3]

We are so wonderfully made that our deepest yearning—to love and be loved—is God's desire for us.

Turning Away from Love

Without knowing it, we turn away from love. It is offered to us every day, moment by moment. Sometimes we embrace love; other times we resist it.

It's easy to understand why. Words sting. Dreams fall apart. Hearts break. To-do lists are long. Time is short. Perhaps someone has wronged you. Maybe you have been excluded, betrayed, or unfairly judged, leaving you feeling lonely or afraid. Perhaps you are dealing with a rebellious teenager or have received disheartening medical tests results. Maybe financial troubles overwhelm you. Perhaps you harbor resentment and are finding it difficult to forgive the pain of an undeserved wound.

I begin many of my mornings immersed in the peace of early dawn. Under the comfort of my covers, I vow I will carry that peace with me throughout the day. I am sure I can do it. I know I can.

Some blessed days actually remain peaceful. I can see the laundry room floor. My husband, Dave, caught the mouse that scurried across the family room the night before. I find my car keys twenty-one minutes before I need to be at an appointment that is a twenty-minute-drive away. I utter "good-bye" just before the battery on my cell phone dies. And I feel like I am at least partially deserving of the adulation I receive on Mother's Day.

Other days, I am jolted from my dream-induced serenity—sometimes within minutes of my feet hitting the floor. Someone tries to control me and I resist; I prefer to be in control. I wound a loved one's spirit with poorly chosen words and have too much pride to make amends. I am not included in an outing; I long to belong. I allow my feelings to be hurt by a person struggling with his own issues, but I suffer in silence rather than work the situation out.

Sometimes, I strive to do better. Other times, in all honesty, I don't try very hard.

What happened to the peace of dawn? I wonder. I am a master of self-sufficiency. I know all about the techniques for getting life "right." I understand I can experience the peace and joy of loving relationships and live with meaning if I try hard enough.

Imagine my surprise when, one day, I discovered the opposite is true. I let my mask drop long enough to learn, in the words of Jesus, "By myself I can do nothing."[4]

My understanding of this—I cannot do it alone—is my best credential for sharing some concepts about relationships and grace on the pages that follow.

A Spiritual Approach

Teilhard de Chardin, a French theologian, said, "We are not human beings having a spiritual experience. We are spiritual beings having a human experience."[5]

Our approach needs to be spiritual rather than a frenzy to do better and accomplish more. Only on the spiritual journey can we experience the profound sense of love and meaning we desire.

Relationships of Grace inspires change from the inside out. It unravels the questions, how do we . . .

- Know God?

- Love ourselves?

- Create loving relationships with others—families, friends, coworkers, neighbors, and acquaintances?

- Overcome fear, worry, stress, addiction, or a bad habit?

- Live with a sense of meaning?

- Open our hearts to grace?

The theme of *Relationships of Grace* is this: You create loving relationships, love yourself, and live with meaning by choosing to open your heart to grace. Note the two keys: grace and choice.

Grace is God's part.

Choice is ours.

The rest of this chapter defines grace and describes the relationships-of-grace approach. The subsequent chapters discuss loving yourself, loving others, living with meaning, the spiritual journey, and growing like a child.

What Is Grace?

Grace is all of the blessings we receive because of God's unconditional love. Grace is the unmerited favor, undeserved mercy, and loving-kindness of God. It is the presence of God, actively working in our lives. Joyce Meyer defined grace on her television show, *Life in the Word,* as "God's power coming to you free of charge to do in your life, with ease, what you could never do with any amount of struggle."[6]

Grace is always present and always free. We cannot earn it and do not deserve it. It is a gift that is given in spite of our imperfections.

Our world is blanketed in grace. All of our blessings and everything good in life flows from God's grace. We could not live without grace; we are totally dependent on it. The air we breathe, the food we eat, family and friends, our talents, and tulips in springtime are all gifts of God's grace. The power of God working through us to help us change and face a challenge is grace. Spontaneous healings, divine incidents, and deliverance from harmful situations are miracles of grace. Lunch with a friend, a walk on the beach, a cozy moment before you get out of bed in the morning, and sitting in front of a blazing fire on a cold winter night are graceful experiences. Even trials that provide us with opportunities for growth and turn our lives around for the good can be acts of grace. During times of weakness, God provides the grace and strength we need when we seek Him.[7] And God's grace—His love, presence, comfort, and power—helps us through.

Grace is not about laws and rules. It is about love and the divine unfolding of love within us. Gerald May, author of *The Awakened Heart,* refers to grace as "love happening, love in action."[8]

A certain amount of mystery accompanies grace. If the definition is not crystal clear, it may be a sign you comprehend the concept more than you realize.

Grace is not an easy term to define—one reference book took six pages, another thirteen. I admire the candor of other authors. One writes he understands grace until he has to describe it. Another gallantly explains he chooses not to define it except through examples.

The concise definition provided here is not intended to be a theological treatise, but rather a brief description of the context in which the term *grace* is used in this book, because opening your heart to grace is key to improving relationships and living with meaning.

Moonbeams of Grace

The moon never shines. It reflects. The sun shines. The sun's rays bounce off the moon and head toward earth. We have come to love the moon's great glow in the sky. Kids look up and search for the face of the Man in the Moon. People fall in love under it. Cows jump over it.

On dark nights when we can't see its glow, the moon is still there and the sun is still shining. Grace always shines, too, even on dark nights, because grace is the presence of God actively working in our lives.

Just as the moon reflects the sun's light, we can reflect the beams of grace if we choose. The New Testament uses the word *administer* when it teaches we should be "faithfully administering God's grace in its various forms."[9] While God is the source, we become vessels of grace when we reflect the rays of love.

Mother Teresa articulated this when she wrote, "Be kind and merciful. Let no one ever come to you without leaving better and happier. Be the living expression of God's kindness: kindness in your face, kindness in your smile, kindness in your warm greeting . . . To children, to the poor, to all who suffer and are lonely, give always a happy smile. Give them not only your care, but also your heart."[10]

As you administer grace to others, you become a moonbeam of grace.

The Naked Choice

Naked and with every hair on their bodies shaved, the room full of men in the Nazi concentration camp were being stripped of everything. The men were given two minutes to undress, drop their clothes in a heap, and throw all their possessions, including wedding rings, onto a blanket. Two minutes and one second later, whips began to crack against their naked bodies. Survivor Victor Frankl described his experience in *Man's Search for Meaning.*[11]

The Nazis intended to attain complete control over their captives. But Frankl made an amazing discovery: No matter how morbid the circumstances, you always have the freedom to choose your response. Despite the dismal surroundings, some men chose to minister to a fellow prisoner, share a piece of bread, or appreciate the beauty of a tree growing outside the prison cell window.

Choice is key to graceful living. Your choice is whether you will allow yourself to be immersed in grace. This is an opportunity you are given moment by moment.

To experience the loving relationships you yearn for, allow yourself to be drawn into the graceful life. Every blessing you have has been given to you. Notice the gifts of grace that surround you—the extraordinary as well as the ordinary. To live in grace is to live soaked in the goodness of God. The Apostle Paul said, "Embracing what God does for you is the best thing you can do for him . . . fix your attention on God. You'll be changed from the inside out."[12] And you will be freed to become a moonbeam of grace by administering grace to others.

You open your heart to grace through a personal relationship with God—*not religion, relationship.* This is a process, not a one-time event. It involves making the choice, moment-to-moment, to enter into a relationship with God.

To live in grace is to allow God's power to work through you. For example, during a speaking engagement, I will be nervous if I try to speak on my own and focus on myself. Will the audience like me? Will they agree with me? Will I do a good job? My stress-level is higher when I strive to remain self-sufficient. But if I lean on God, ask Him to help me, and focus on the message rather than the outcome, my anxiety will diminish.

By speaking in partnership with God (albeit not an equal one), words will be given to me. Yes, I need to practice and prepare, but I am not speaking alone. I have a Helper—which also means the applause is not mine.

It is freeing to realize the goal is not perfection. What's important is living into God's plan. God will give you the grace you need if you are willing to receive it.

To choose to receive grace is to know God and experience a profound inner peace. Turning away from grace and resorting to self-sufficiency results in emotional turmoil. You are free to choose to live the peaceful, graceful life no matter what you are struggling with: for example, fear, a challenging task, hurt feelings, low self-esteem, envy, a difficult person, anger, temptation, forgiveness, a bad habit, lack of patience, stress, addiction, uncertainty, or health problems.

How do you open your heart to grace, moment by moment, through choice? Enter into a relationship with God. Develop an awareness of the blessings of grace given to you. Move from striving on your own to allowing God's power to work through you. Let God work His will in you. Ask Him for help. Relinquish self-sufficiency, recognize your dependence on, surrender to, and trust in God. And leave the outcome to God.

In short, know God.

Then, God will transform you.[13] He will change you from the inside out by changing your heart.

Change your heart and you change your life.

You know God.

Your relationships improve.

You love yourself.

You fear less.

You live with a sense of meaning and purpose.

God offers you the choice, but will not choose for you. You are free to accept or reject the standing invitation to live in grace.

Reach for His hand. Dance to His music. Bask in His love.

In graceful moments, the longing of the heart is satisfied. As you enter into the miracle and mystery of grace, you will create loving relationships, love yourself, and live with meaning.

You will experience relationships of grace.

CHAPTER TWO

Loving Yourself

A propane lantern fascinated a man who lived in a hut in an African village without electricity or modern conveniences. He spotted the lantern while shopping in town, bought it, and brought it back to his village.

Its flame pierced the darkness one night. The unfamiliar glow drew his village neighbors. The man carried the lantern into his hut, but was not happy with what he discovered. The lantern illuminated the dirt inside.

He complained to his wife about the dirt. Again and again, he complained. Finally, she gave him a choice: the lantern or her.

We don't like people to see our dirt. We all have it, and we spend a lot of time and energy trying to hide it.

But you are infinitely more than your imperfections. I know because I read about you. Your description is in the number-one bestseller of all times: the Bible. I didn't have to read far before I found the narrative about you. You are in the first chapter of Genesis, "So God created people in his own image; God patterned them after himself; male and female, he created them."[14]

My reading about you did not stop there. I found you in the Psalm that says God "crowned us with glory and honor."[15]

Do you know how marvelous you are? You are created in the image of God and crowned with glory and honor.

To be created in the image of God does not mean we are perfect or gods. God is always greater. But one of the remarkable things about grace is God loves us despite our dirt, although God doesn't always love the things we do and wants us to make healthier choices.

"I'm So Glad I'm Me"

"I'm so glad I'm me," my daughter, Erin, joyfully proclaimed one day when she was young. No inhibitions. No self-consciousness. It was just a simple expression of her love for life and herself.

Loving yourself is Biblical. The Golden Rule and the Great Commandment to "love your neighbor as yourself" are based on the assumption you love yourself.

Self-love is not to be confused with being self-centered. Self-love leads to selflessness and self-sacrifice. It does not mean "me first;" it means "me *too*." Self-love does not mean you neglect your family and friends to get what you want. It means you do not neglect yourself in the process of loving others. It is not a prideful arrogance. Humility increases as self-love grows. Self-love develops out of a reverence for God's creation and by understanding you are valuable to your Creator, despite your flaws.

When you love yourself, you are more loving toward others. Your relationships are better with fewer conflicts. You are able to make healthier choices. Criticism is not as disabling. Adverse circumstances and other people's opinions do not easily sway you. You feel more joyful and at peace. Instead of resenting other people's good fortune, you can rejoice, secure in the knowledge there is plenty of grace to go around.

Our Need for Love

Mother Teresa said we are created "to love and to be loved." Love is our deepest desire, our greatest passion. Every person ever born longs to love and be loved. Self-love is critical for healthy relationships and personal growth. Our ability to love others is directly related to our ability to love ourselves. When I am not feeling good about myself, it impacts my relationships with others. Internal hurts wound those around me.

We cannot give what we do not have. When we are critical of ourselves, we are critical of others. When we are filled with rage, we lash out at others. But when we are filled with grace, we are free to respond in grace to others.

People with a low sense of self-worth often feel hurt and make unhealthy choices. People who have been disabled by past experiences of abuse and abandonment have an especially difficult challenge. Some wounds are so deep that turning to God is the only way to heal.

Difficulties in our relationships with others often stem from personal issues. Many personal problems can be traced to a lack of self-love. Some people fight. Others flee. Some become doormats, allowing people to take advantage of them, and try to pacify others or solve their problems. Others engage in self-destructive activities.

Many people expect others to make them happy instead of accepting responsibility for their own happiness. They look to others to fill their emptiness and make them whole. How they feel about themselves is dependent on external circumstances.

Love from others is never enough. To use a common example, if you fill a bucket with water, but the bucket has a hole in it, you can pour water in the bucket all day and never fill it. You must first plug the hole.

But how is the hole plugged? How do you love yourself? That is the subject of this chapter.

Self-love grows, not through an endless search into self, but through grace—by accepting God's love and nurturing a personal relationship with Him. This means trusting in that which is greater than self and making the choice, moment by moment, to accept the gift of God's grace.

You were created in the image of God.

God loves you unconditionally despite your dirt.

You are of value because God created you.

You were given unique talents to love and serve the world around you.

Because value is not a function of dirt, this does not mean ignore the dirt because God will love you anyway. But as you accept God's love, you will behave more lovingly because you will be transformed.

We'll explore how you can embrace your inherent value as a person created by God as we discuss:

- The Mask, the Mud, and the Masterpiece

- From Fear to Love

- Value from Birth

- Overcoming the Fear of Other People's Opinions

- Darkness Into Light

- Integrity

The Mask, the Mud, and the Masterpiece

A tornado threatened the home I was visiting when I was a child.

My family was vacationing with friends in Ohio's heartland, as we did every summer, when a tornado warning sounded. With a taut upper lip, our host scrambled to open the cellar doors and prepare for our refuge into the cellar.

Watching Auntie Em do the same for Dorothy on TV every year was the closest to a tornado I had ever been.

Fortunately, that tornado never struck, but I witnessed the aftermath of one that did. The path of destruction was distinct, exactly as I'd always heard it described. A line of devastation was clearly visible as I looked across the city. Three adjoining houses sat among the wreckage of shattered glass and uprooted trees with their roofs blown off. The neighboring houses escaped the ruin. A friend working in the basement of a warehouse was unaware the funnel-shaped cloud had touched down a block away.

The whirling wind pummeled the side and back walls of one house to the ground. The front was left unscathed. The house appeared normal from the front, but the back of the house was a pile of rubble.

The façade masked what lay behind it.

The Mask

We, too, have a façade that masks what lies beneath. It is the front we put on for others. The mask tries to deceive and hides the person within. It is concerned with what other people think. It worries about projecting the right image to the world. The mask tries to make us look good. It tries to show how great we are and that we are better than another person. It tries to prove our worth by showing how smart, talented, and wonderful we are. Our desire to be number one, belong to the best group, and achieve power and wealth are the mask at work.

The mask associates worth with doing and having. Feeling good is dependent on *doing* well in school, on the job, in sports and *having* possessions, power, control, and the admiration of other people. Unhappiness is the result of not being able to *do* or *have* something we want.

The mask tries to hide the mud.

The Mud

The mud is our fear, envy, insecurities, discontentment, resentment, and concern about what other people think. It is the part of us that tries to conform to the world. Unhealthy and unloving choices are made in the mud.

Self-discovery can be difficult because it exposes the truth: We all have mud. I am wedged in it up to my waist sometimes.

We try to circumvent our vulnerability by denying our emotions. Rather than feel our pain, we mask it. Some lash out in anger rather than admit they are hurt or afraid. Others try to escape by anesthetizing their pain. They turn to substitutes like shopping, alcohol, food, work, or unhealthy relationships.

Loving Yourself

But what we *want* is different from what we *need*. The cravings are for something deeper, something more.

Saint Augustine of Hippo said long ago, "We keep searching until we find ourselves in God." Everything flows from this longing. Nothing else can bring us into the fullness of life. When I am trying to "find myself," self gets in the way if my search is independent of God.

The basic component of mud is self-sufficiency. We spend a lot of time in the mud when we are out of relationship with God.

What keeps me from loving myself? Not accepting God's love. Wanting things my way instead of trusting God to provide what I need. Insisting things happen my way, on my timetable, on my terms. Trying to control other people and circumstances instead of accepting them as they are. Languishing in the mud.

A sign of spiritual maturity is growing in awareness of how deep the mud is, while at the same time turning to God for help and marveling that He loves us anyway.

My husband, Dave, and I bought an antique table that is painted green. It is a nice shade, but green, nonetheless. The ornate trim encircling the table is also layered in green paint. Dave used to refinish furniture in a wealthy area outside of Philadelphia; he knows wood. He knelt down and discovered underneath the painted green façade is a gorgeous, solid black walnut table. Someone had chosen to hide the table's natural beauty, the black walnut, by painting it green.

When waddling in mud, the mask does the same thing. It covers your natural beauty. It hides the love within, your likes, dislikes, vulnerabilities, and special talents for serving others.

Beneath the green paint, our table is black walnut. Beneath the mask and the mud is a masterpiece longing to be unveiled.

The Masterpiece

The sculpture *David* is ready for a bath. His last bath was 129 years ago. Ulysses Grant was president. It will take seven months to swab the dirt away.

Michelangelo sculpted the statue from a slab of marble some believe Leonardo da Vinci once owned. The statue depicts the legendary Biblical character that slew the giant Goliath with a single stone and cut off his head using the giant's own sword. It stands sixteen feet ten inches tall and weighs nine tons.

Michelangelo said *David* was already in the slab of marble. His job was to unveil the masterpiece within.

The Apostle Paul wrote, "We are God's masterpiece,"[16] God's work of art.

The statue of *David* is Michelangelo's masterpiece. You are God's.

Graceful Strategies

Let's consider the following strategies for letting go of the mask, moving out of the mud, and unveiling the masterpiece:

- Allow the masterpiece to be unveiled.

- Live as the person you were created to be.

Allow the masterpiece to be unveiled

How do you put down the mask and get out of the mud? How is the masterpiece unveiled?

The answer is simple. You don't unveil it. God does. Your part is choosing to accept the gift of grace and to know God.

While creating *David,* Michelangelo said it was his aim to release the angel imprisoned in the stone.[17] God's aim is to release the angel in you and set you free from the bondage of self-sufficiency.

In Romans, the Apostle Paul urges, "Give your bodies to God. . . . Don't copy the behavior and customs of this world, but *let God transform you* into a new person by changing the way you think. Then you will know what God wants you to do."[18]

To "give your body to God" is to give all of yourself to Him. Instead of conforming to the world, put God at the center of your world. Then, God does the work of transforming you.

Change is through transformation, not imitation.

The mask is too tough to penetrate and the mud is too deep for you to change all by yourself. By accepting the gift of grace, you allow God's power to work in you. This helps you risk moving from "I want what I want" to trusting in what God wants.

The masterpiece is unveiled as you are shaped by God's hand when you choose to enter into a personal relationship with Him. As the masterpiece is unveiled, you become the person you were created to be. The longings of your soul are satisfied. Your choices are healthier and more loving as you move out of the mud and become anchored in grace.

Unveiling the masterpiece is a process, not a one-time event. God is gracious; we see glimpses of the masterpiece even when we choose to turn away from grace. But as you move deeper into relationship with God, moment by moment, the marble is chiseled from cold slab to become a masterpiece.

Live as the person you were created to be

Thirty copies of the *Declaration of Independence* were printed and distributed for review throughout the thirteen colonies. Six of the original thirty were lost, presumably destroyed. Twenty-four original copies remained.

31

A man bought a painting at a garage sale for five dollars in 1989. He noticed a tear in the back of the painting. Out of curiosity, he removed the painting from its frame and discovered the twenty-fifth original copy of the *Declaration of Independence.* In 1991, the man sold it during a Sotheby's auction for $2.1 million. It resold a few years later for $8.1 million.[19]

On the *Antiques Road Show,* people are often surprised at the appraised value of their "junk."

Another man who shopped at garage sales every Saturday bought an old painting he liked for fifty dollars. Hard times struck. The man lost his job. Needing to eat more than he needed the painting, he sold it for "lunch money." The painting, he discovered, was the original work of a renowned painter. The sale price? $1.5 million.[20]

One person's junk is another person's treasure. One person's passion is another person's frustration. One person's strength is another person's weakness.

You were uniquely created with special gifts. Your strengths, the things you love to do, and the things that fill your life with meaning are divinely inspired.

After you have entered into a relationship and "let God transform you into a new person . . . *then* you will know what God wants you to do."[21] *Then* you will understand your identity as a person created by God to love and be loved, and to use your unique gifts for God's purposes. *Then* you will be free to accept yourself, love yourself, and live as the person you were created to be.

Discovering what brings you joy includes understanding what keeps you from it. Self-destructive activities that drain your energy and prevent peace are signals that your choices are inconsistent with the desires of your heart.

To discover your longings, complete the sentences below.[22] Contemplate the words of Soren Kierkegaard, in *The Prayers of Kierkegaard,* "And now Lord, with your help I shall become myself."[23]

- I experience joy when . . .

- I feel at peace when . . .

- I can nurture my spirituality by . . .

- The blessings of grace that surround me are . . .

- I have fun when . . .

- My strengths are . . .

- My weaknesses are . . .

- I would like to be remembered for . . .

- If I keep living as I am today, I will be remembered for . . .

- My top five priorities in life are . . .

- The qualities I admire in other people are . . .

- The qualities I admire in myself are . . .

- I can use my talents to serve others by . . .

- The thing I love most about my life is . . .

- The thing I am most dissatisfied about in my life is . . .

- Things that drain my energy are . . .

- I am enthusiastic about . . .

- Time passes quickly when I am . . .

- Time passes slowly when I am . . .

From Fear to Love

During a vacation to St. Petersburg, Russia, my family and I listened in wonder as a woman we had met hung her head and told us the story of her grandfather.

During Stalin's rule, her grandfather entertained a friend in his home one evening. At the kitchen table, they enjoyed some vodka, each other's company, and a few laughs.

During the merriment, they exchanged jokes. I don't know if her grandfather had too many swigs, but it seems he told one joke too many. In the gaiety, he made a joke about Stalin, a big no-no behind the iron curtain.

In my family, I'm famous for telling jokes where the only person who laughs is me. Perhaps this grandfather was the same way. Apparently, her grandfather's friend did not think the Stalin joke was funny. The friend turned in his host to the KGB; he was probably afraid not to.

Strange men burst through the door of her grandfather's home the next day and seized her grandfather. Tragically, the family never saw or heard from him again.

For those of us who have grown up in the United States, this is hard to understand. "Hello FBI, so-and-so told a joke about the President." "Hello, CIA. Did you hear the one about . . .?"

Stalin's was a reign of terror.

It is hard to envision, but Stalin was also afraid. He feared going to sleep in his own bedroom. He took turns sleeping in seven different rooms out of fear of being assassinated. He traveled in a motorcade with five limousines with curtains drawn so no one knew which limousine carried him. A servant guarded the teabags to make sure nobody tampered with them.[24]

Stalin was afraid.

We are, too.

Fear

Public speaking has been ranked as the number one fear in many studies, above illness and death. Comedian Jerry Seinfield jokes that the average person would rather be in a casket than give a eulogy. The real fear is not public speaking. It is what people will think of us.

A certain amount of fear is healthy. Fear warns us of potential danger and signals us to take action in threatening situations. It is important to heed these warnings. Fear keeps a woman from walking alone at two o'clock in the morning and a child from accepting candy from a stranger. Fear of getting hurt keeps us from running out in front of a moving car. Fear of the consequences keeps us from engaging in self-destructive activities.

What triggers some of our other, less rational fear? We want to belong. We want to feel special and know we are loved. We seek power and control. Consider some examples of fear that stem from our desire to be in control and our need for security and love.

- A man does not pursue his passion because he fears the unknown.

- A woman stays in a job she is bored with because she is afraid to leave her comfort zone.

- A man becomes a workaholic because of his fear of failure.

- A woman is immobilized by criticism because she fears she is unloved.

- A man boasts about his charitable works because of his fear of not being good enough.

- A woman argues to prove she is right because she is afraid of not appearing smart enough.

- A man reacts with hostility because he is afraid to admit he is hurt.

- A couple spends beyond their means because they fear not being held in high esteem by their friends.

- A man overeats and a woman shops to mask emotional pain because they are afraid of letting their feelings show.

- A man acts without integrity because of his fear of people's opinions.

- A woman stays in an unhealthy relationship because of her fear of being alone.

- A man envies his friend's achievement because of his fears about his own self-worth.

- A woman seeks power because she is afraid to release control.

We are all afraid at times—of loss of security, of loss of control, and of not being loved. We are afraid because we know along with love comes hurt.

The Wizard of Fear

Who can forget the wizard whose reign was one of fear? The International Wizard of Oz Club can't. The club dates back to 1957 and is still active today. Thirteen hundred members reside in twelve different countries. Oz events are celebrated at festivals and at the annual Ozmopolitan and Munchkin conventions. *Oz* magazine, Oz auctions, and an Oz trading post help keep the memory of the classic story alive.[25]

The story is memorable. After journeying into deadly poppy fields and down the Yellow Brick Road into Oz, Dorothy longed for home.

With knocking knees and a heavy heart, Dorothy, the small and meek, asked Oz, the Great and Terrible, for help. She received her orders: If she ever wanted to see Auntie Em, Uncle Henry, and a Kansas wheat field again, she had to kill the Wicked Witch of the West.

Dozens of Winged Monkeys and one melted Wicked Witch later, Dorothy returned to the Great Wizard with her friends: the Scarecrow, Tin Man, and Cowardly Lion.

Back inside the great throne room, Toto exposed the truth with one pull of the curtain: The Wizard was a fake. The Great Wizard was a little man with a wrinkled face and bald head. In an instant, Oz, the Great and Terrible became Oz, the Great and Terrible Humbug.

Perhaps it was prudent for Dorothy's initial approach to the mysterious Wizard to be cautious. Fear alerts us to threatening situations and prods us to establish boundaries. But in the end, Dorothy had nothing to fear.

Our fears are usually unfounded as well.

"Fear not" passages are included in the Bible 366 times—a verse for every day, including leap year.[26]

What are the consequences of fear, and how do we "fear not"?

Consequences of Fear

Consider the ways fear can be destructive:

- *Fear keeps us from loving.* We cannot fear and love simultaneously. Fear robs us of our peace.

- *Fear keeps us from leaving the security of our comfort zone to become the person God created us to be.* Fear can keep us stuck in an unhealthy relationship or in work that is inappropriate for us. Pursuing our passion and living with a sense of purpose requires us to trust God to provide what we need as we follow His will.

- *Fear keeps us from surrendering control.* Instead, we struggle for power over people, things, and circumstances we cannot control.

Every behavior serves a purpose. What is the payoff of fear?

One of the functions fear serves is to mask the person hiding beneath the surface. We are afraid of becoming vulnerable and exposing the real us. We are afraid of what people might think if they knew the person behind the façade.

Like the wife in the African hut with the new lantern, we prefer to hide our dirt. We toughen the shell, paint our black walnut green, and create an armor of protection to hide what's beneath the surface. Rather than admit we are hurt or afraid, we rage. We blame others, become defensive, and exile the people who threaten us.

Perhaps a bigger fear is that *we* might see past our façade. We are afraid of what we might find if we look too deep. We try so hard to project a certain image that we lose sight of who we really are. Or, perhaps we do know who we are, but we are afraid we are not of value.

The irony is, along with the mud, the mask hides the most beautiful part about us. The mask hides the angel, the masterpiece longing to be unveiled.

Longings of the Soul

Much of what we do is an act of love or a cry for it. Love and hate are antonyms according to the dictionary. But the root of hatred is fear. Emotions that appear to be unloving or hateful are masking fear.

Fear-based emotions and behaviors include: resentment, envy, anxiety, embarrassment, pride, self-centeredness, a compulsion to control or be controlled, arrogance, defensiveness, insecurity, hostility, habitually proving you are right, and a compulsion to please.

To grow past our fear and move deeper into love, it helps to understand who we are as individuals.

People identify themselves in a variety of ways—through their work, family, hobbies, achievements, etc. But these are experiences. They are not who you are.

Our self-descriptions are incomplete when we seek identity through roles, activities, and accomplishments. What we *do* is different from who we *are*.

Our true identity is a person uniquely created in the image of God to "love God, neighbor, and self."[27] Understanding who we are grows out of our understanding of God's will and by using the gifts given to us for God's purposes.

Different methods of personality typing attempt to categorize people according to personality traits, highlighting vast differences among us. But among the diversity is a greater similarity: our need for love. When you walk into a room, you can already know the profound longing of every person there—a yearning for love.

The commandments to love God and one another are teaching you to follow the longings of your soul. By first seeking your deepest longing—God—you will then move away from fear and deeper into love for neighbor and self.

Graceful Strategies

Let's consider the following strategies for moving from fear to love:

- Surrender control.

- Know you are equally special.

- Trust.

Surrender control

I shuddered as I dove into the icy water during my first lifesaving class when I was a teenager. The instructor wanted to teach the students how to save a drowning person. I swam like a fish, straight toward the "victim."

My stint as a would-be hero was brief. The first lesson jolted me as much as the frigid water: I would likely drown with my approach-from-the-front technique. In his panic, the drowning person is likely to grab his rescuer, pull him underwater, and drown both himself and his rescuer. The safer approach for the rescuer is from behind, out of sight, and underwater.

A drowning person often struggles for control—when his path to survival is through surrender.

Similarly, when we are drowning in the mire of self-sufficiency, the graceful path is through surrender.

The key is to surrender control, not to another person, but to God. God is our rescuer. When you surrender control, you "let go and let God" and "cast all your anxiety on him."[28] You allow yourself to be drawn into grace through a personal relationship with God. You take off the mask and give up the fight of self-sufficiency for the promise of peace.

Surrender is accepting God's will and yielding our will to His. Surrender involves trusting God without knowing the details of His plan.

Fear keeps us from surrendering. When we are afraid, we fight. We strive to prove our worth. We struggle for security. We seek control.

When we surrender, we stop wasting our energy. We stop trying to control people and circumstances over which we have no power anyway. We acknowledge the pain instead of engaging in unhealthy behavior. We listen and understand rather than defend or attack.

Surrender does not mean you avoid personal responsibility, give up, stay in bed all day, or become a doormat. Nor does it mean you allow another person to control you. Establish limits and resolve conflicts, but in love.

It took one pull of the curtain for Toto to expose the Wizard as the Great and Terrible Humbug. Truth eventually triumphs.

The truth is God is in control. Surrender happens, not by trying harder, but by understanding and resting in this truth. Surrender is not easy, but it is key to letting go of fear.

Know you are equally special

Many people make it to the doctor when they discover a lump in their breast. Jerri Nielsen, M.D., made headlines when she performed a biopsy on herself, diagnosed cancer, and self-administered chemotherapy while stranded at the South Pole, which was inaccessible because it was the dead of winter. She was there performing research and was the only doctor on the continent of Antarctica.

In *Ice Bound,* Dr. Nielsen wrote about the lessons she discovered as she battled cancer in the darkness of a South Pole winter. One of her most memorable was the equality of everyone who wintered together in the desolation of the South Pole.

Initially, Dr. Nielsen thought the people with "type A" personalities would be the problem-solvers. Living inside during six months of darkness changed her thinking. Dr. Nielsen noted when a type A was "pacing like a lion," the type B's calming effect helped the group through the darkness.[29]

Traditional hierarchies disappeared. Each person's unique gift was critical for survival. In her role as doctor, Dr. Nielsen explained she might help one ailing person feel better. But without the mechanic who serviced the generator, every person could die. Should the generator stop working, the mechanic had two hours to fix it and restore power in temperatures of one hundred degrees below zero.

Every member of the research team was important. No one person was more important, or better, than anyone else.

You and I are part of a team—humanity. The Master Craftsman molds each of us. Each of us is specially made— uniquely created with extraordinary talents—but of equal value to everyone else.

Part of overcoming fear is giving up the fight to prove how special we are. When we seek to be more special, to be better and of greater value, we put ourselves at the center of the world. It is freeing when we no longer feel the need to prove we are better than those with whom we share this earth, but know we are special to the One who created it.

You are special to God, regardless of how special the world may or may not think you are. No matter what issues you are struggling with, no matter what you may or may not have accomplished, no matter what indiscretions lurk in your past, you matter to your Creator. Being better than others is not what makes you special. You are special because you are His.

Trust

When Moses was instructed to bring the Israelites out of Egypt, God said, "I will be with you."[30] After Moses' death, God commanded Joshua, "Do not be afraid or discouraged. For the Lord your God is with you wherever you go."[31] The same truth applies to us today. "I will be with you" is all we need to know.

Moving past our fear requires us to leave the security of our comfort zone to live God's plan, and trust in Him to provide what we need.

The antidote to fear is faith.

Meister Eckhart, a Dominican mystic of the thirteenth and fourteenth centuries, said all of nature seeks the path on which God might be found. We are spiritual beings. Our hearts keep yearning until we journey into a relationship with God.

Living spiritually is more than practicing good values. Spirituality is connectedness with the divine. It is being willing to enter into a relationship with God and trust in His goodness.

John, the disciple, taught, "There is no fear in love. But perfect love drives out fear."[32] God is the source of perfect love. Love triumphs over fear in moments when we experience divine intimacy and trust in God's perfect love.

Love is not a means to an end, not a way to manipulate life toward happiness. Love is the end itself. We choose love for love's sake, not because of moral obligation, but as the response of a transformed heart.

How can you fear less and love more? How can your need for security, love, and control be met? Trust God. Accept and administer grace, by accepting God's love and allowing that love to flow through you. Release things and place them into God's hands. When the world seems to be falling apart, the security that can come only from God will bring you peace.

The antidote to feeling unloved is to love.

Value from Birth

Please excuse me, but I'm frustrated. My e-mail is down. I caused the problem, with a little help from some magnolias. Three bouquets of sapphire, cream, and magenta adorn my home. Their elegance rises twenty-eight inches above a cherry-wood table and a slate-gray marble mantel.

I'm especially fond of the sprays because I created them. Being a novice at flower arrangement, I must confess, I am a bit proud of my handiwork. I snapped some digital photos to send to my mother, my sister Vickie, and a friend. They are the only people on earth I thought might be remotely interested. I loaded the photos onto the computer and attached them to an e-mail.

One click of the mouse later, my troubles began. The photos used too much memory and locked up the computer system. The corrupted e-mail had to be deleted before the system would work again. But first, I had to find the tainted message. Apparently, it was out in electronic la-la land somewhere. Have you ever tried to communicate with a dot-com company via e-mail when your e-mail is down?

Back to my flowers.

Are my floral arrangements perfect? Not even close. One is lopsided. Another is asymmetrical. The third suffers from floral gap.

Do I love them anyway? Absolutely. Are they beautiful? Dazzling. Why did I create them? To enjoy them. I see one arrangement right now. *Sigh.*

Why do I love them? Because I cared enough about them to create them.

How about you? Is there something you created that you love, not because it is perfect, but because it is yours? Perhaps it was a craft, a creative solution to a problem at work, a gourmet dinner, or some woodworking. Can you relate?

Back in a minute. My e-mail is up; I've got mail.

The Reason You Are of Value

I love my flowers because I created them and they are mine. God loves you because He created you. And He wants you to be His.

God created you for the same reason I created my flower arrangement: for enjoyment and pleasure. God is gleeful about you. If you don't believe me, read the Psalm, "God delights in his people."[33]

You are valuable because God cared enough to create you. Not perfect, but valuable. Value is a gift of grace. You are of value to your Creator because you exist. You are not required to *do* anything for this value. You cannot earn it. You cannot lose it. I delight in my flower arrangements because I created them. God loves you because He created you.

Value is not an entitlement. You are of value, not because you have earned your worth, but because God is love. God is always greater. God's love is so extravagant your innate value is given freely as a gift. Understanding you do not have to be perfect—cannot be perfect—but are of value anyway makes the gift of grace even more remarkable.

Consider the synonyms of the word *valuable. Important. Treasured. Cherished. Esteemed. Precious.* In other words, *loveable.* My flowers are all of these.

You are, too.

Who Me? Yes, You.

After I taught one of the first Creating Loving Relationships classes, a woman approached me with a pen and paper in hand. "I want to write down something you said," she remarked. I had mentioned a few of my favorite quotes during the class. One by one I repeated them.

"You mean the one about . . ."

"No, not that," she answered.

"You mean this one . . .?" I asked.

"No," she replied.

"Was it the one about . . .?"

"No."

Puzzled, I racked my brain. The only other person left to quote was . . . no, it couldn't be. The person she was seeking to quote could not possibly be *me.* But it was. She wanted to write down something I had said. As I repeated the quotes of the gurus, it never crossed my mind that the words this kind lady sought were my own. I did not understand her comment was directed toward me.

Sometimes it is hard to comprehend the truth of some profound words that are also directed toward me—and you: God loves you.

Allow me to repeat it in case you missed it: God loves you.

Who me?

Yes, *you.*

We have all heard the words *God loves you.* It is another matter to grasp their magnitude. It is easier to comprehend *you* in the plural sense, when it is directed to all of humanity. But in this case, *you* is singular.

God loves *you.*

You.

YOU!

You are magnificently created, specially crafted. Your heart pumps the blood that delivers nutrients and oxygen to every cell in your body and lugs away the waste—in twenty seconds. Your brain is more powerful than the fastest computer, looks like a three-pound sponge, and is made of one hundred billion neurons that would span 250,000 miles if placed end to end. In spite of us sharing these qualities with others, we are all still unique beings created in God's image. Amazing.

Beings not Doings

The victims of one of the September 11, 2001, plane crashes were listed in a newspaper article. Business titles followed their names. Curiously, titles did not appear after every person's name. Only "notable" titles were published. Lawyer. Financial trader. Television producer. Human *beings* whose lives had been tragically cut short were being reduced to what they *did*.

We tend to measure self-worth based on performance. When we associate value with accomplishments and doing, we sacrifice love for achievement.

When value is tied to doing, perfection becomes the standard. My flower arrangements are far from perfect and have no achievements on their résumé, but I love them anyway. Perfection is a standard we place on ourselves. Just how good is "good enough"? God never expects us to be perfect and loves us anyway. Recognizing the reality of our imperfection provides the opportunity for accepting grace.

God's capacity to love is greater than our capacity to mess up. Yes, we are held accountable and suffer the consequences of poor choices. Self-responsibility is a major theme of the Bible, but so is the unfailing, unconditional love of God.

As we are drawn into the mystery of God, we are freed to appreciate how loveable we are in God's eyes in spite of our imperfections. Efforts to make God love us are futile because God never stopped loving us in the first place.

In *What's So Amazing About Grace?*, Philip Yancey writes, "Grace means there is nothing I can do to make God love me more, and nothing I can do to make God love me less. . . . God's love comes to us free of charge, no strings attached."[34]

You are a human *being*, extraordinary because you *are*. Achievements, good deeds, and the accumulation of material possessions are not a barometer of value.

Made some unhealthy choices? Wounded by someone else's misconduct? Spouse mad at you? Mess up at work? Such issues have no effect on your worth. You are valuable.

Receive a promotion at work? Wear designer clothes? Adept at what you do? Your child at the top of his class? You are undoubtedly blessed, but your worth remains unchanged.

Your acceptance of your inherent value and God's unconditional love is key to self-love.

The concept of being of value from birth could be used as an excuse to be lazy and do nothing. But the opposite occurs when you understand your intrinsic value. Self-worth is mobilizing.

When you accept grace and know God, you will do good works because you want to when your heart is transformed. By all means, do good deeds. But do them because it is the right thing to do, not as a means of earning your worth.

Graceful Strategies

Let's consider the following strategies for recognizing you are valuable from birth:

- Understand the value of God's creation.

- Enter into a personal relationship with God.

Understand the value of God's creation

Feelings of low self-worth happen when we fail to acknowledge that *everything* comes from God. Loving God involves loving everything God has created, including you. Self-love is not an emotional attachment to personal worth. It is reverence for that which God has created.

Loving yourself is a faith issue. If you believe in God as the Creator, present in the miracle of birth, your value is an inherent part of creation. To deny this is to deny the value of God's creation.

The question, then, is do you believe in God as the creator? If so, do you acknowledge the value of His creation?

If someone tells me, "God loves you," who is doing the loving? God, not me. If I am already struggling to love myself, it can be difficult to comprehend I am the recipient of this love.

But answering the question "do you love God's creation?" calls for an active response, a choice, on my part. I am the one being called to choose love.

We seek love but we ignore the Greatest Love of all.

The sacred landscape is too overwhelming, too grand, and too incomprehensible. It is difficult to appreciate the magnificence of something so vast we can never fully understand it. The closest thing we can liken divine love to is parents' love for their children. Parents love their children just because they were born. No matter what their children do and what mistakes they make, parents' love is steadfast.

Remember the man in Africa who brought a lantern into his hut? He didn't like the dirt. God loves you, dirt and all.

You are loveable, not because of your accomplishments, but because of your Creator.

God loves *you* unconditionally. God breathed life into *you*. Among the splendor of the universe, God invested in *you*. God chooses *you*.

Do you love God's creation?

Enter into a personal relationship with God

Self-love grows when you enter into a personal relationship with God and accept His love. Saint Augustine of Hippo said God continually tries to give good things to us, but our hands are full.[35] Moment by moment, you are given the opportunity to choose whether you will open your heart to grace. This means taking the risk to be more spiritually connected by recognizing your dependence on God and surrendering control to Him.

Grace penetrates the deepest pit.

When you allow yourself to be drawn into grace, you know God, not through knowledge but through a relationship. Pain from the past begins to heal, and you are transformed. Your love for God's creation, including love for yourself, grows. This means you don't try to earn God's love, but accept it as the gift it is.

You are of value because God created you.

Overcoming the Fear of Other People's Opinion

Stop with me for a moment and think about these questions: [36]

- Do you feel guilty when you say no?

- Does criticism crush you?

- If someone is mad at you does it ruin your day?

- Are you afraid other people will not like you?

- Do you do things you don't want to do because you are afraid someone might not like you if you don't?

- Are you afraid people will think you are incompetent?

- During conflicts, do you cry and apologize when you are not at fault?

- Is being "nice" more important to you than doing what you know is right?

- Do you have trouble standing up for yourself?

- Do you quietly seethe rather than face an issue?

- Do you go to great lengths to win someone over who is upset with you—not because it is the right thing to do, but because you are afraid he or she will stay mad at you?

- Is it difficult for you to assert yourself?

- Are you a people-pleaser?

- Do you allow others to disrespect you?

- Do you allow others to take advantage of you?

- Are you afraid to discipline your children for fear they might get mad at you?

- Are you so busy pleasing everyone else you have no energy left for yourself?

- Do you go along with things to get along when it is contrary to your value system?

Yes answers to any of these questions may mean you, like most people, fear other people's opinions of you.

Fearing Other People's Opinion

Love and belonging are basic human needs. This makes us vulnerable to the opinions of others.

We fear other people's opinions of us. We want to be liked. Most of us get anxious if someone is mad at us, so we:

- Say yes when we should say no

- Trade honor for acceptance

- Value being nice above being safe

- Weep instead of working it out

- Burn out instead of taking time out

- Throw in the towel instead of standing our ground

Putting other people's needs above our own is seen as a virtue in our culture, especially for women who are taught to be the nurturers and to be "nice" at all costs. Some people run themselves ragged doing things for others while ignoring their own physical, spiritual, and emotional needs. Most likely this is done out of fear, not love. What would others think if we asserted ourselves or took time out to tend to our own needs?

Service to others is crucial when gifts are given joyfully from the heart. Done begrudgingly, it leads to bitterness, resentment, and burnout.

The Unavoidable Problem

Jesus taught, "You have heard that it was said, 'Love your neighbor and hate your enemy.' But I tell you: Love your enemies and pray for those who persecute you,"[37]

Did you notice the unavoidable problem? Jesus did not teach we should not have enemies. He assumed we would. Therein lies the problem. We are going to experience the disapproval of others.

Growing Stronger

Our need for love and belonging is so fundamental to our existence that we will never be able to completely overcome our fear of the opinions of others. It's nice to be admired, but it is not possible to receive the approval of everyone with whom we come in contact. If a person claims to be immune to other people's opinions, he or she may be attempting to become invincible by denying the human need for love and belonging.

Your worth as a human being is in no way dependent on winning the approval of others. Disapproval does not decrease your worth. Approval does not increase it. You are of value because God cared enough to create you.

Will other people recognize our value? It's unlikely. They may perceive some value if we are wealthy or in a position of power, but only as long as the money and positional power lasts.

We can continue growing so we are not overly sensitive or immobilized by feelings of rejection. As you grow, we will experience less emotional turmoil. Criticism will not hurt as much. Conflicts will be resolved more quickly.

Graceful Strategies

Let's consider the following strategies for overcoming the fear of other people's opinion:

- Accept that a certain amount of disapproval is inevitable.

- Don't give another person power over you.

- Change your focus from people to grace.

Accept that a certain amount of disapproval is inevitable

Leaders throughout history experienced the disapproval of others: Christ, Gandhi, Nelson Mandela, the Dalai Lama, and Dr. Martin Luther King, Jr. were targets of hatred. Why? They were value driven and stood firmly in their beliefs. You've heard their stories. They peacefully fought against injustice. But many people disapproved of them. These teachers of love were the recipients of hatred. Christ was crucified. Gandhi and Dr. Martin Luther King, Jr. were assassinated. Nelson Mandela spent twenty-seven years in prison. The Dalai Lama was exiled from his homeland.

The message? A certain amount of disapproval is inevitable. Expecting everyone to like and approve of us all the time is unrealistic.

Don't give another person power over you

Many of our most celebrated leaders who suffered injustice could have avoided their fate but they chose not to. Why? They would not allow their enemies to have power over them. They stayed focused on their beliefs and refused to give in to the disapproval of their enemies.

Authentic power is grace, God's power, flowing through you. Your worth is not affected by the opinions of others.

Change your focus from people to grace

My husband, Dave, is a daredevil. I am not. But because I am married to him, in an effort for togetherness, I have experienced adventure. I've slithered through two-foot openings to explore caves. I once flew in a sailplane, an aircraft without an engine. I've dangled off the end of ropes, scaled rock walls, and stepped backward off the edge of seventy-five-foot cliffs to rappel down them. Today, I wonder why anyone would want to step off the edge of a cliff.

One crisp fall day, Dave and I went rock climbing in the mountains of West Virginia. The sun illuminated the tapestry of reds, oranges, and yellows blanketing the mountains. It was one of those days you are glad to be alive, and I preferred to keep it that way. That's why my heart was thumping.

We were on the exposed ledge of a steep drop. The climb itself was not rough, but the plunge would be if I missed my footing. Dave put me in a belay, meaning he tied a rope around me, secured it, and held the end of it. Should I tumble, Dave would break my fall because he was hanging onto the other end of the rope.

As soon as I hooked into the rope, my heart resumed a regular beat, and I climbed to the mountaintop with ease. I did not work at becoming less fearful. But I was no longer afraid because I had placed myself in Dave's hands.

Whenever you have a mountain to climb, God extends His hand to help you. And He is there to break your fall.

John the Disciple wrote, "The one who is in you is greater than the one who is in the world."[38]

Place disapproval from others in God's hands. Ask what lesson can be learned from the situation. Focus on God's will instead of human will. You will grow from the experience.

Rejected by a family member? Accept the invitation to enter God's family.

An unsupportive spouse? Let God support you.

A critical boss? Receive the unmerited favor of God.

In the graceful life, you place yourself in the hands of the Great Protector holding the other end of the rope. Your focus changes from the people in the world to the Creator of the world.

And one day you realize you are not as afraid of the opinions of others.

Darkness Into Light

Thirty thousand feet up something smelled funny—to the flight attendant, at least.

"Do you smell smoke?" she asked as I waited in the line that forms at the lavatory in the back of the plane after a meal is served.

I didn't.

"Smell the lavatory," she said. This was not an experience I anticipated when I paid for my ticket. Something about smelling a lavatory made me feel ill at ease.

Obediently, I sniffed. The flight attendant explained: People in first class smelled smoke.

The flight attendant pounded on the door. No answer. She pounded again. And again. Still no answer.

Wide-eyed, I watched her next move. Out came the key. In went the flight attendant.

"Put it out," she commanded.

Sheepishly, a man emerged. He looked about fifty years old with hair longer than my daughter's. He confessed: He disabled the smoke detector to sneak a cigarette. The four-hour plane ride was more than he could endure.

What he thought was done in the safety of darkness came into light.

Because air circulates throughout the cabin, the smoke was carried from the rear of the plane to the first-class section. The people in front smelled what those of us on sniff patrol in the back could not. Interesting.

The man returned to his seat. The flight attendant called the authorities. And I, well . . . I'll end my story here.

Meaning by Way of Suffering

Sometimes it takes a lavatory door busted open and the threat of a two-thousand-dollar fine to help us learn.

Our tendency is to look outward to other people and external circumstances for the solution to our problems. If only he were a better mate (or friend, or relative, or boss), things would be peaceful. If only circumstances were different, my problems would be solved. If only I could get the new job and a bigger house, life would be good.

Expectations are one of the greatest deterrents to joy. They indicate we assume someone or something else is responsible for our happiness. When other people or external circumstances don't turn out as anticipated, we become hurt, angry, disappointed, or irritated. The greater the expectation, the greater the hurt.

We are the walking wounded. Sometimes our pain is the consequence of our choices. Other times pain is inflicted upon us through no fault of our own. Either way, we ache and wonder why.

Suffering exists. Jesus is referred to as the Suffering Servant. The reality of suffering is the First Noble Truth the Buddha taught. The Second Noble Truth is suffering happens for a reason.

Abraham Lincoln grew up in poverty and lost several elections before he became president.

Ludwig van Beethoven was deaf when he wrote some of the world's most beautiful music.

Michael Jordan was cut from his junior high school basketball team.[39]

Baseball great Babe Ruth held the world record for the number of homeruns hit as well as for an incredible .847 batting average. He set a world record during the 1918 World Series when, over several games, he pitched twenty-nine innings without a single run being scored. But Babe Ruth held another record. He struck out more than any other major league player.[40]

When Thomas Edison was experimenting with the lightbulb, he threw the switch thousands of times only to find the bulb would not light. Edison considered these experiments successes, not failures, because he learned another way the bulb would not light.

Sometimes our greatest problem is not the dilemma itself, but losing hope. That is when we are most likely to let a problem defeat us.

The Beauty of Aging

I gazed in wonder upon the maples and aspens one perfect autumn day. They radiated shades of crimson and gold upon the cloudless, azure sky. The vibrant hue of leaves freshly fallen blanketed the landscape.

The sun warmed my back as I ambled in the cool, crisp air beside mountain streams. Although I was alone, I was far from lonely.

I was witnessing the alpha and omega, the beginning and the end. From life to death, the leaves descend upon the earth. Their nutrient-rich mulch stimulates new growth as they decompose.

Immersed in the brilliance of autumn, I reflected upon the irony. Leaves are most beautiful just before they die. Our culture would have us believe only the young are beautiful, but falling leaves teach us otherwise. We are here to learn the way of love. Like autumn leaves upon the ground, we are most beautiful just before we die. My friend once read, "It is not your fault if you are not beautiful at eighteen. It is your fault if you are not beautiful at eighty."

What is the beauty of aging? Growth. Wisdom. Love. And, hopefully, trust.

Graceful Strategies

Let's consider the following strategies for moving from darkness into light:

- Seek grace in the darkness.

- Lean on God.

- Ask, "What am I being called to learn?"

- Trust God.

Seek grace in the darkness

One of the most surprising aspects of grace is it is often hidden in turmoil. Personal hardship, frustration, boredom, irritations, encounters with difficult people, financial difficulties, and burnout can all be acts of grace. Sometimes we have to crash before we are willing to slow down.

The Disciple Peter wrote, "Think of your sufferings as a weaning from that old sinful habit of always expecting to get your own way. Then you'll be able to live out your days free to pursue what God wants instead of being tyrannized by what you want."[41]

We all experience pain. Some people are faced with horrible suffering and inexplicable pain. Sometimes we find ourselves so far down in the pit, it is hard to imagine we will ever be able to climb out.

The temptation is to try and figure out why bad things happen to good people. Trying to make sense out of suffering is one of the most difficult aspects of our faith walk. But logic can work against us because it keeps us from trusting in God.

Who can explain hardship and tragedy? According to Scripture, we should not try. "Lean not unto thine own understanding," Proverb commands.[42] As a friend says, it helps to understand we will never understand.

Please be aware, it is not my intent to trivialize pain. Our hurts are real and, well . . . painful. But hear the hope of Romans, "In all things God works for the good of those who love him, who have been called according to his purpose."[43]

In *The Hiding Place,* Corrie ten Boom said, "Every experience God gives us, every person he puts in our lives, is the perfect preparation for the future only He can see."[44]

Darkness precedes growth. Sometimes, God may bring us face to face with an obstacle until we learn. This is not to imply evil is God's will. Evil is the result of human will—free will—and wrong choices. But learning the way of love is a growth experience, although growth is not always in the direction of our choosing.

The Apostle Paul had what he referred to as a thorn in his flesh. Paul never revealed the specifics of his ailment, but he divulged its purpose: "to torment me" and "to keep me from becoming conceited." Paul begged to have the thorn removed, but God told him, "My grace is sufficient for you, for my power is made perfect in weakness."[45]

It would have been easy for the prolific author of much of the New Testament to become arrogant and forget about his need for God. The Lord wanted Paul, not puffed up, but on bended knee—and mindful of his dependence on God. So God added a thorn to the mix.

Problems are not hopeless situations. They are messages. Heartaches and mild depression can be signals telling us we are ready for passage into a new phase. A broken romance may indicate it was not a good match. A home that does not sell might mean it is not the right time to move. Feelings of isolation can teach us to reach out to others. Exhaustion is a sign to rest. A difficult person challenges us to examine our own behavior and ask how we might be contributing to the conflict. Anguish in a job can reveal we have chosen the wrong career. A pattern of toxic relationships may suggest we need to learn who people are by watching what they do, rather than listening to what they say.

Lean on God

Trust in the words spoken to Paul: *Grace is all you need.* Paul was most likely to turn to God during times of weakness. By relinquishing self-sufficiency and receiving grace, Paul allowed God's power to work through him. Paul became stronger than he ever would have been if he relied on his own strength.

God is always at work, even—especially—in our brokenness. As we search among the ugliness and pain, we will experience grace if we risk being open to it.

At our lowest points, when we are feeling vulnerable, we are often most willing to reach through our brokenness to the merciful grace of a loving God.

The Psalm eloquently says, "If your heart is broken, you'll find God right there; if you're kicked in the gut, he'll help you catch your breath."[46]

Lean on God. Ask for the strength and wisdom to make the right choices. Heavy burdens lighten when you rest in Him. God will help you through.

Ask, "What am I being called to learn?"

When a tragedy occurred, psychoanalyst Carl Jung is reported to have said, "Let us open a bottle of wine. Something good will come of this."[47]

Darkness comes before light. Pain is a signal something is out of balance and you have choices to make. By adapting a paradigm of finding the lesson, you transform problems into opportunities for learning and growth.

Many of life's most important lessons are based in paradox. Common expressions teach us this.

- Some good comes from bad.

- A weakness can make us grow stronger.

- A painful experience can be a powerful teacher.

- The more we give, the more we receive.

- The line between joy and pain—and love and hate—is thin.

Scientific studies show plant growth is greater during stormy weather than sunny weather.[48] The storms of life help people grow.

As we grow, we heal. Individual healing becomes world healing in aggregate. When you view problems as learning experiences, they become opportunities for growth—the bigger the problem, the greater the opportunity.

Aborigines in central Australia speak of "mysteries not yet revealed to mortal man," explains Marlo Morgan, in *Mutant*

Message Down Under. They believe you must "take the test to pass the test" and strive to "close the circle of each experience" leaving no "frayed ends." If you "walk away with a bad feeling," that experience will be repeated until you learn the lesson.[49]

God will give you the grace you need to pass the test. The Apostle Paul said, "No test or temptation that comes your way is beyond the course of what others have had to face. All you need to remember is that God will never let you down; he'll never let you be pushed past your limit; he'll always be there to help you come through it."[50]

If you break open the head of a flower about to reseed, you will find many seeds preparing to begin a new life. Many seeds will fall, but only a few will germinate into a flower.

We are continually given seeds for growth. Viewing problems as learning opportunities helps you detach emotionally. Troubles become opportunities for learning. Bruises heal into understanding and insight.

At age ninety-five J. C. Penney said, "My eyesight may be getting weaker, but my vision is increasing."[51]

As an author, it is uncanny how often I experience a problem the same day I am writing about it. When writing about judgment, I might have a bout with judging. When writing about fear, I might experience anger that masks a fear. These are gifts, calling me to firsthand learning, to better prepare me for translating lessons into words.

We were created to be in relationship with one another. As we love, we will experience pain. Pain is a part of love. Suffering is a part of the human experience.

A healthy psyche does not make me immune to grief or feelings of rejection. It gives me the courage to ask, "What might I be doing to invite suffering? What is the lesson I am being called to learn?" Paul's lesson was to learn how to keep his pride in check and rejoice in his need for grace.

When angry, hurt, or upset, I am free to ask . . . [52]

- What am I being called to learn from the "thorn in my flesh"?

- Am I leaning unto my own understanding instead of trusting God?

- What is the purpose of my behavior or emotions?

- What is the payoff?

- What do I want that I am not getting?

- Am I so focused on getting what I want that I'm ignoring the other person's needs?

- Am I trying to control circumstances instead of accepting reality?

- Am I being trained for a future not yet known to me?

Trust God

We all like to be in control. It starts young. Watch any two-year-old.

A friend's son thought he would show her who was boss one day when she instructed him to do something. Striving to maintain control, this thirty-inch captain of the sandbox shouted, "no!" He then grabbed his backside and backed against a wall as protection for what he knew was coming.

Such struggles for control go all the way back to Adam and Eve in the Garden of Eden. God gave them everything they needed. But they wanted one more thing to make their life complete: the fruit from the tree that gave knowledge of good and evil. They wanted security. They wanted power, control, and knowledge. They thought they knew best.[53]

Don't we all like things to happen our way, on our timetable, and on our terms? Don't we like to believe our way is best?

Our expectations keep us struggling to mold the perfect family, be number one, obtain recognition in a certain way, and prove we are right. Our constant striving for one more fruit keeps us from loving ourselves, others, and God.

Unmet expectations cause a lot of our pain. But the things we wish for, and pray for, are not always what we need. "Be careful what you wish for," the saying goes. "Thank goodness I have not been given everything I have asked for in my prayers," is the old tongue-in-cheek joke.

The graceful life is about trust. When we surrender, we give up control and turn things over to God. This does not mean we abdicate self-responsibility. It means we stop trying to control things over which we have no control anyway.

Think of a boat anchored when a storm strikes. Darkness descends upon daylight. The wind gusts. The seas rage. Whitecaps swell. Waves crash upon the shore. The boat thrashes around on the rough seas. Things inside it clatter and clang. But the anchor holds. The storm passes.

The boat endured. It weathered the storm. Some paint may have chipped. A piece of glass might be cracked. The boat suffered, but it persevered. New dings add to its character as a well-traveled vessel and bring with it the hope of future journeys. All because the boat was securely anchored.[54]

What keeps us from loving ourselves and from being securely anchored? Unmet expectations. Insisting things happen our way instead of trusting in God's plan. Not accepting God's love and grace. Separating ourselves from God.

Trusting is difficult. One of the reasons trusting is difficult is that often we do not understand why things happen, why the storms hit. Who can explain suffering and heartache?

Trust means we are willing to place our problems in God's hands and surrender our fears in faith.

When we trust that which is greater than us, God is our anchor. This allows us to move into a more loving way of behaving. We believe the Psalm, "[God] will give you the desires of your heart."[55]

Trusting is key for moving from darkness into the light.

Integrity

September 11, 2001, was a day of extremes most Americans will never forget. We saw the worst and the best of humanity that day. Among the debris, angels emerged. Many told their stories.

People fleeing down the stairs from the top floors of the World Trade Center met firemen on the fifty-second floor—running up.

A man stayed with his quadriplegic friend on the twenty-eighth floor to hold the phone for him while he called his wife.

Men carried a fallen priest for blocks to place him on the altar of a church.

A fireman who sifted through the rubble looking for survivors found, and carried out, his own son.

Teachers in a day-care center in the World Trade Center complex put toddlers into shopping carts and ran with them for hours to safety. Men on the street ripped the shirts off their backs and gave them to the children to shield their faces from the ashen air.

Men carried a woman in a wheelchair, whom they had never met, down sixty-eight flights of stairs.

Heroes on Airline Flight 93 faced evil men wielding box cutters to save the lives of people they did not know.

Were they afraid? Undoubtedly. Did the man who held the phone for his quadriplegic friend tremble as the flames drew near? I suspect he did. Where did the incredible firefighters get the courage to run up the stairs? Did they see the faces of the

children they would no longer hold or the spouse they would never again kiss? Perhaps.
Ordinary people doing extraordinary things.
Remarkable.
Amazing.
Integrity.

What is Integrity?

Dwight L. Moody, an American evangelist, said, "Character is what you do in the dark." I would say that integrity is choosing your thoughts and actions based on values rather than personal gain. Ethics prevail above individual benefit. Decisions consider the best interest of everyone involved. Interactions with others are compassionate.

In *The Three Little Pigs,* the pig that built his house out of bricks on a solid foundation withstood the affront by the big bad wolf. When you live with integrity, choices are based on the foundation of truth and moral standards.

The prayer of integrity is God's will be done.

Integrity heals. Lack of integrity hurts. The fact that "everybody else does it" or "nobody will know" is irrelevant. Personal satisfaction, expectations, and the fear of judgment are beside the point.

Integrity is compromised any time the best interest of everyone involved is not accounted for. Biblically, gossip, fighting, greed, envy, and arrogance share the list with murder.[56]

Self-Respect and Self-Love

Author Mark Twain said, "Few things are harder to put up with than the annoyance of a good example."

Integrity is key to self-respect, which grows when our actions are consistent with our value system. We lose self-respect when our actions are inconsistent with our values.

Self-respect affects the way we feel about ourselves. Acting with integrity increases our level of self-respect and feelings of self-love. When we lack integrity, we do not feel good about who we are; our sense of self-worth diminishes.

Ungraceful Consequences

A man who owed money was feeling a twinge of guilt over his lack of integrity. He decided to pay some of his debt to ease his conscience. He sent some money along with a note: *I couldn't sleep so I am sending you $100 of the money I owe you. If I still can't sleep, I'll send you the rest.*

An attorney told me it is not uncommon for him to find the perpetrators of unethical business dealings in the hospital with stress-related illnesses. When you are out of integrity, your conscience records and remembers it.

People who administer lie detector tests receive Christmas cards from prisoners expressing gratitude for the relief they felt after they confessed.[57]

What are the consequences of lack of integrity? When the clerk gives us too much change, what is the problem with keeping it? Do we really "get away with it" when we pad our expense account, gossip about our neighbor, or distort the truth?

The problem is we remove ourselves from the loving state of grace. The consequences can be painful. We experience inner turmoil: regret, anxiety, guilt, shame, and sorrow.

Our relationships with ourselves, other people, and God suffer.

We hurt our relationship with ourselves because we lose self-respect, thereby, diminishing our feelings of self-love.

We hurt our relationships with others because we lack credibility with them. People don't trust us and distance themselves from us. Feelings of guilt and shame may cause us to distance ourselves from them as well.

We hurt our relationship with God because our heart wants to choose God's will. To act without integrity, we either separate ourselves from God or we were not in a relationship to begin with. When we are in a relationship with God, we choose integrity.

Graceful Strategies

Let's consider the following strategies for living with integrity:

- Never allow another person to compromise your self-respect.

- Allow the power of grace to flow through you.

Never allow another person to compromise your self-respect

Gandhi said, "They cannot take away our self-respect if we do not give it to them."[58] By choosing actions based on an ethical center, you do not allow another person to compromise your dignity and self-respect. Choice is key.

Allow the power of grace to flow through you

Living with integrity is difficult. The consequences are often painful. It is not easy to stand in truth when it may cost you something you want: for example, some extra change, a friendship, or your job.

How do you find the courage and strength to live with integrity? By being filled with the power of grace, through a personal relationship with God.

Human strength is no match for the power of grace.

CHAPTER THREE

Loving Others

A black bear joined Dave and I for dinner one night. A real one. I'll affectionately refer to him as "Yogi."

I have a few things in common with the black bear species. They, like me, have an insatiable appetite; can gorge until their stomach is close to bursting; prefer a vegetarian diet of greens, berries, and nuts to mammals; and ferociously protect their cubs. But I digress.

Like a ghost, Yogi descended upon Dave and my campsite on the edge of a forest in the Canadian Rockies. Yogi wandered in with his head down below his shoulders, a stance that signals aggression in bear language. Not exactly what I hope for when I open the door for a dinner guest.

Our three-hundred-pound friend had a smooth, short-hair, chocolate-brown coat. His jet-black eyes and fiery gaze looked right through me. His paws grabbed our sixty-pound cooler and flung it as if it were empty.

Yogi rose to his hind legs on the picnic bench, doubling his height, as he feasted. A roll of paper towels and a brown grocery bag were the appetizers. One thump of the cooler later, the lid sprung open and dinner was served. The main course was anything within reach. Edible or not. It made no difference.

With trembling hands and a pounding heart, I shot a roll of close-ups from the other side of the picnic table. I snapped them from the comfort of our truck, where I sat with the engine running—an important advantage since the species has been clocked at speeds up to thirty-five miles per hour. Upon our safe return home, my nephew Matthew, who was three at the time, was gleefully enthralled with the pictures and brought them to preschool for show-and-tell.

Living with Bears

Any bears in your life?

Maybe the bear in your life is bald instead of furry or has well-manicured paws. A bear is a bear, nonetheless. Perhaps a family member gives a lot of unbearable advice but not many bear hugs. Maybe a boss' favorite thing to chomp is you. Or a friend salivates as you eat some humble pie.

At a management seminar I attended, the instructor asked us to list our most difficult problems in the workplace. We students called out our woes as the teacher wrote them on a white board.

The instructor stood back and reviewed the list. Relationship issues not only topped the list, they were the only problems on it. The instructor, who had taught the class for years, noted the difficulties mentioned were always people problems.

Meaning Through Relationships

Stanford University did a study of breast cancer patients on the benefits of being in a loving environment, surrounded by loving people. The results were significant: The survival rate was twice as high for the group in a loving environment. They stopped the study; it would have been unethical to subject the control group to an environment with such reduced odds of survival.[59]

We long to move deeper into the fullness of loving relationships. We feel isolated and lonely without them. Unresolved issues in our relationships create turmoil. Our connections with one another bring meaning into our lives.

The challenge is to recognize we are dependent upon grace for peaceful, loving relationships. Too often, we demand love rather than offer it. We grow by learning to accept and administer grace.

But how are we to cope with the bears in our lives that are attracted to the smell of garbage and rotting fish? "Don't feed the bears" literature is given to visitors in national parks inhabited by bears. Forest service rangers teach, "Respect the bears." Rangers describe black bears as shy. They attack only when they are provoked or feel threatened—precisely when human bears are most likely to attack.

We'll explore how you create loving relationships with others as we focus on:

- The Holy Spirit

- The Golden Rule

- Acceptance

The Holy Spirit

It must have been our lucky night. A friend and I had gone out to dinner. As we left the restaurant, my friend, who was driving, was able to make an easy left out of the parking lot, even though we were in the middle of a busy city.

The traffic light we came to half a block later was not signaling. No red. No green. Not even a flashing yellow. Being an astute driver, my friend stopped at the intersection, anyway.

Our internal warning system sounded as we looked into the darkness and across the intersection. Out of the shadows, five sets of headlights illuminated our faces. We had turned the wrong way on a one-way street.

The light turned green. The wall of headlights, five lanes across, flocked toward us. The car straight ahead flashed its blinking red lights—a police car. The only problem for us was he was going the right way, and we were headed in the wrong direction.

Holy Guidance

The Holy Spirit helps you turn in the right direction. God works within and communicates with you through the Holy Spirit. Because of the Holy Spirit, you are able to experience God's presence and have a direct relationship with Him. The Bible refers to the Holy Spirit as your Counselor, Comforter, and Helper.[60] The Holy Spirit helps you when you are weak, shows you God's will, and teaches you what to say.[61]

Willpower is not enough to effect change. You need the power of grace, working through the Holy Spirit, to change.

When you listen to the Holy Spirit, you are listening in the presence of God. Father Thomas Keating, a founder of Contemplative Outreach, likens listening to the Holy Spirit to a pilot using one of the old airplane guidance systems.

Pilots navigated by following radio beacons strategically placed on major air traffic routes throughout the country. These stationary radio beacons emitted signals. A plane's navigation system picked up the beacon's signal as the plane flew toward the beacon. If the plane began to stray off course, the signal faded. By monitoring the signal strength, a pilot knew when he was beginning to veer off course and could reposition to get back on route.

The Holy Spirit is our divine guidance system. The Holy Spirit beacons us to stay on course and helps us find our way when we lose our bearings. We often look outward to others for guidance when many of our most important answers lie within, through the Holy Spirit.

Fruit and Consequences

The Holy Spirit guides us to accept and administer grace.

When we don't listen to the Holy Spirit, we make a lot of wrong turns, as my friend and I did the night we faced the flashing red lights of a police car. Instead of being vessels of grace, we stop its flow when we don't allow God's grace to flow through us. The moonbeams of grace lose their glow. We choose poorly causing us to feel shame, guilt, and remorse. Our relationships suffer. We experience regret, hurt, and disappointment. Decisions are difficult. Our feelings of self-respect diminish.

As you open your heart to grace and enter into a personal relationship with God, the Holy Spirit will transform you. This is a choice you must make. You will then be filled with the Spirit. The Lord told Ezekiel, "I'll give you a new heart, put a new spirit in you. I'll remove the stone heart from your body and replace it with a heart that's God-willed, not self-willed."[62] Then, you will reap the fruit of the Spirit: "love, joy, peace, patience, kindness, goodness, faithfulness, gentleness, and self-control."[63] Your relationships will improve. You will feel better about yourself. You will fear and worry less. And you will live with a sense of meaning, purpose, and passion.

Graceful Strategies

Let's consider the following strategies for living in the power of the Holy Spirit:

- Listen, surrender, and trust.

- Choose peace and fairness.

Listen, surrender, and trust

People have trouble pronouncing and spelling my last name: *Karcher.*
"Archer with a K," I explain.
"Kar*t*cher," they write.
"K-archer," I respond.
"*C*archer," they write.
I spell it, "K-a-r-c-h-e-r."
I watch them write, "K-a-r-*t*-c-h-*n*-e-r."
They are not deaf. They hear, but are they listening?
To live the graceful life, we are radically dependent on listening to, surrendering to, and trusting in the Holy Spirit. This is a moment-by-moment choice. Our problem is not lack of wisdom; it is lack of trust. We hear but we do not listen. We

know but we do not believe. Surrender frightens us because it means giving up control.

We are not as powerful as we think we are when it comes to working out our lives. Much of what happens is beyond our control. While we always have a choice about how to respond in a given situation, we cannot control external circumstances.

Calling on the power of the Holy Spirit helps you administer grace. An "I can do it myself" determination changes to a prayer—"I cannot do it alone, please help." This helps you move into a more loving way of behaving. God gives you "the power to do what pleases him," according to Philippians.[64] Of course, this assumes the person doing the asking and listening has a healthy conscience and is of sound mind; this will not work for someone with an unhealthy conscience or a sociopath.

Proverbs says, "Listen for God's voice in everything you do, everywhere you go."[65]

How do you know what you hear is God's voice working through the Holy Spirit? Sometimes it's not easy to know. It took a burning bush to get Moses' attention. Theologian John Wesley said, "Do not hastily ascribe all things to God. Do not easily suppose dreams, voices, impressions, visions, or revelations to be from God. They may be from Him, they may be from nature, they may be from the devil."[66]

A friend's fiancé identified himself by both first and last name whenever he called her, even though they were engaged. My friend and I found this amusing. Why? Because when you have a close relationship with someone, you learn to recognize his or her voice.

When God is your friend, through a personal relationship, you will recognize His voice more readily. God may communicate with you in a variety of ways: Scripture, prayer, feelings of peace, physical discomfort, "coincidences" (divine incidents), the words of another spoken at just the right

moment, a page in a book, music, nature, and daily incidents—
both ordinary and extraordinary.

Choose peace and fairness

Choice is key. The Holy Spirit guides you and works within
to effect change. Your part is to make the right choices and
trust in the power and wisdom of the Holy Spirit to help you do
what is right.

How do you know if your choices are consistent with the
guidance of the Holy Spirit? Again, it's not always easy to
know. The Holy Spirit guides you to choose peace and
fairness; you will be able to answer *yes* to all of the following
questions if the Holy Spirit is providing the guidance.[67]

- *Is your choice consistent with God's Word? Is it consistent
  with love and God's commandments?* Because God works
  within you through the Holy Spirit, guidance will be
  consistent with Scripture. This is the greatest test of all.

- *Are you comfortable with your choices?* Incorrect choices
  create discomfort. Pay attention to inner turmoil. It may
  indicate you are on the wrong path and need to find a better
  solution. Granted, the right choices are sometimes
  uncomfortable, but you should feel a quiet conviction about
  your choices, even during times of conflict.

- *Does your choice lead toward peace?* The Holy Spirit
  guides you toward peace, kindness, love, and conflict
  resolution. Choices are based in love, not fear. Behavior
  shifts toward peace and away from arguing, gossip,
  judgment, putting on airs (success, money, status, power),
  having to prove you are right, excessive competitiveness,

seeking the approval of others, maintaining a hectic lifestyle, and living without meaning or purpose.

- *Does your choice account for the best interest of everyone involved?* The Holy Spirit will guide you to be kind but firm, and choose what is right. The Holy Spirit will not guide you in a manner that is self-destructive or insensitive toward others. Sometimes we promote our own interests and neglect the other person's. Other times, we respect the other person's best interest but neglect our own. Sometimes we are nice—not for altruistic reasons—but because we are afraid of saying no. The Holy Spirit accounts for the best interest of everyone involved.

- *Are the consequences fair?* Evaluate the consequences. Are they acceptable? Are they necessary? Are they fair? If not, work to find an alternative solution. Consequences are not always pleasant, but they should be just.

The Golden Rule

Blood revenge was practiced in primitive times as part of ancient society's custom of retribution. The adage that became the Golden Rule to treat others the way you would like to be treated dates back to the fifth century B.C. It reflected the popular ancient ideal of reciprocity.

The concept was quickly transformed into guidance for controlling reciprocity. It became an appeal for mutually kind behavior. "An eye for an eye" was intended to curb revenge so retaliation was not worse than the initial offense. It was also a law of equality to ensure the master received the same retribution as the slave, the rich the same as the poor. Jesus later linked the Golden Rule to the radical concept of loving your enemies.

The Rule

All major religions teach some form of the Golden Rule:[68]

- *Christianity:* "Do to others what you would have them do to you."[69]

- *Buddhism:* "Hurt not others in ways that you yourself would find hurtful."

- *Confucianism:* "What you do not want done to yourself, do not do to others."

- *Hinduism:* "Do by the things of others as they do on their own."

- *Islam:* "Desire for your brother that which he desires for himself."

- *Judaism:* "What you hate, do not do to anyone."

- *Taoism:* "Regard your neighbor's gain as your own gain and your neighbor's loss as your own loss."

Karma or Grace?

Some compare karma to the Golden Rule, but they are not the same.

Common expressions teach the principle of karma. "What goes around comes around." "You get what's coming to you." "A man reaps what he sows."[70] "For every action there is an equal and opposite reaction."

Karma is both your actions and the consequences of your actions in the form of an energy force. According to the principle of karma, your actions create a flow of energy that comes back to you in similar karma.

According to the principle of karma, every action has a consequence. You receive what you give. Compassion sows kindness. Cruelty reaps malice.

Karma is more than your actions. It includes motivation. "Good karma" requires positive motivation and actions. When motivation is negative, the belief is "bad karma" is created, even if actions are positive. People sometimes refer to this as "bad vibes." Negative karma would be created if you harbor feelings of hostility or give a gift resentfully, even if you are not overtly impolite.

In Hinduism and Buddhism, the belief is karma creates ethical consequences that determine your destiny in your next life when you are reincarnated. The effects of karma accumulate over time. The goal is enlightenment— transcending karma by freeing yourself from negative karma through personal choice. Proper thoughts and actions enable you to reach a state of nirvana in Buddhism or *moksha* in Hinduism. According to the Hindu and Buddhist belief, this puts an end to your suffering and brings you freedom from reincarnation's cycle of death and rebirth.

The Christian belief is salvation is through faith by grace. We will never be able to "achieve" enlightenment no matter how hard we try, and that is precisely why we need grace. God's grace is given freely as a gift; it is not earned through works. Consequences and reaping what you sow are consistent with Christian teachings, but for the ultimate purpose of bringing a person closer to God, not to balance a karmic scorecard.

Grace is a gift of unconditional love. Karma is a principle of conditional love. Grace offers the hope of undeserved mercy and unmerited favor. Through grace, we receive extravagant blessings we do not deserve and infinitely more blessings than we give. The scorecard never balances. To paraphrase author Philip Yancey, the math always works out in our favor.

The Golden Rule teaches us to administer grace to others, as we would like others to give grace to us.

Golden Living

Bill W., cofounder of Alcoholics Anonymous, resorted to a pull-them-off-the-barstool approach in the early days of the AA program. He was passionate about helping people stop drinking.

But the barstools remained full and Bill W. became discouraged. He told his wife he had failed; nobody had abstained. But his wife observed *he* had not had a drink since he started trying to help others quit.

Helping others became one of the twelve steps.

Isn't it marvelous how we are made? When you help others, you help yourself. A man makes it his mission to help alcoholics stop drinking and, in the process, he abstains. Ben Franklin said, "When you are good to others, you are best to yourself."

Living the Golden Rule is more than an obligatory moral response. It is what your heart longs to do. The Golden Rule is more than a behavioral guide. It is an appeal for you to be yourself, a person created to love and be loved. In the graceful life, you are transformed from the inside out. You are motivated to do the right thing simply because it is the right thing to do.

Thomas Aquinas, philosopher and theologian of the thirteenth century, said, "Sin is not disobedience of irrational authority, but the violation of human well-being."[71] Struggling against the Golden Rule is painful. We sacrifice love for achievement, winning, and personal gain.

Graceful Strategies

Let's consider the following strategies for living the Golden Rule:

- Develop a heart for God.

- Give what you want to receive.

Develop a heart for God

When asked which commandment is greatest, Jesus quoted from Deuteronomy, " 'Love the Lord your God with all your heart and with all your soul and with all your mind.' This is the first and greatest commandment. And the second is like it: 'Love your neighbor as yourself.' All the Law and the Prophets hang on these two commandments."[72]

Notice that loving God comes first. This is not for God's sake; it is for ours. When we love God, we experience a transformation of the heart. Only with a changed heart, one that has been molded for God, do we have any hope for loving others.

The Golden Rule calls us to consider the impact of our behavior on other people. I cannot do this on my own, but if I seek that which is greater than me, God will help. Self-responsibility is important, but I am not the only one at work. This involves taking a moment to pause, ask, and listen. Pause to remember God. Ask for guidance and a heart open to grace. And listen for God's reply.

Grace allows you to rest a little if you lean on God. When you ask Him to help, God will give you the grace you need.

Graceful living involves seeking God everywhere—in ordinary daily events, in our interactions with other people, and during times of conflict. Our only hope of loving our neighbors as ourselves is to receive God's grace and allow His grace to flow through us to other people.

We are continually called to open our hearts to grace. Our need for grace is much like our need for water—our survival depends on it, and it is not enough to drink only once.

Receiving grace is a choice that must be made from moment to moment.

Give what you want to receive

Two words summarize the Golden Rule: give grace. God is the source of grace. But we become vessels of grace when we choose to open our hearts to it. Become cognizant of the choices you make. Every encounter is an opportunity to administer grace.

A friend starts each day with a prayer that she can help someone that day with a smile, kind words, or a hug. Each gift is free.

The amount of love in your life is dependent on you, not other people. If you want more love in your life, act more lovingly. If you want to be treated with kindness and compassion, treat others with kindness and compassion. If you want others to accept you as you are, accept them as they are. If you want to be fed, feed the hungry.

This is easier said than done. It calls you to forgive the unforgivable, love the unlovable, and be gracious to the graceless. It means you hate injustice, but love your foe as you contest unfairness. You may loathe an institution, but love the individual running it. During conflict you respond firmly, but kindly, with dignity and grace. This does not mean you let people take advantage of you. Protect yourself and others from harm and hold others accountable for their actions, but do so in grace. Rather than returning "evil for evil," you are called to break the cycle of what author Phillip Yancey refers to as "ungrace."

Acceptance

Lying on the ground after a forty-foot fall, the emergency workers examined Grandfather for signs of life. As they whisked Grandfather to a hospital, Dad opened the door to a policeman who had come to deliver the news, "Your father has been in a terrible accident . . ." My father, twelve years old at the time, was later told by well-meaning hospital staff to prepare to take care of his family.

Grandfather was a roofer. He had been working on a mansion in the city. A fellow worker fell off the roof onto the scaffolding where Grandfather worked. The other man was unhurt, but he knocked Grandfather off the scaffolding, down a forty-foot drop onto some concrete steps.

With most of his bones broken, his teeth knocked out, and severe internal injuries, Grandfather was not expected to live. For four long months, he lay in a hospital bed and struggled to survive.

Miraculously, he recovered and was written about in medical journals. It was the 1930s. He was one of the first people to have metal plates surgically implanted to draw his bones together and help them mend.

I never once heard Grandfather express an unkind word about the fellow who nearly cost him his life. I never heard him complain about the months of excruciating pain he endured in the hospital bed.

I wonder if I could have been as gracious and accepting.

95

Disunity

Accepting people as they are is easy—as long as no people are involved.

One of the nicest things about writing is I can pontificate all day and everyone in the room agrees with me. A week of writing and my computer does not talk back once. I'm the boss. King of the keyboard. Ruler of words . . . until it goes in for editing.

It's tempting to try and change people, to get them to see things our way. Who can blame us? On *Father Knows Best,* Betty, Bud, and "Kitten" always believed father really did know best. Television housewives of the 1950s and 1960s cleaned in pearl necklaces. *The Brady Bunch* merged six kids at the height of puberty from two divorced families without a hitch. The Walton brothers and sisters never went to bed without a "Good night, John-Boy."

Read the challenge to which we are called: "If anyone says, 'I love God,' yet hates his brother, he is a liar. For anyone who does not love his brother, whom he has seen, cannot love God, whom he has not seen. And he has given us this command: Whoever loves God must also love his brother."[73]

What's wrong with not accepting people as they are? The fundamental problem is disunity. We experience hostility, judgment, and fear. We bicker and seek control. Disunity brings us out of relationship with one another. It makes it impossible to "love our neighbor as ourselves."

Acceptance is . . .

Some people have rats for pets. I never knew this until an acquaintance told me the story of hers. She has some acreage, where she keeps a horse, a goat, a chicken, and a pet rat. Her kids were not feeding the rat, so she opened the front door and let it go.

The rat ran to the barn and made it his new home. He doesn't need the kids to feed him anymore; he eats the chicken's food.

A man went out to the barn to care for my friend's horse one day. She followed a couple of minutes later. Wide-eyed, the man met her at the barn door to alert her of the rat. As he forewarned her, the rat climbed up her body and sat comfortably on her shoulder.

"Weird," the man muttered.

The goat perches on the horse's back. The chicken sits on top of the goat as the goat sits on the horse. Then, the rat climbs to the top of the heap and sits on top of the chicken that is on top of the goat that is on top of the horse.

That's what I call unity.

Here's my question: If a horse, a goat, a chicken, and a rat can live in harmony and accept one another, can't we?

Acceptance is the ability to choose peace regardless of external circumstances.

What are the benefits of acceptance? Harmony, peace, and joy. Before we can love one another we have to accept one another. We don't all share a common viewpoint, but we can all share a common grace.

Acceptance is not . . .

Acceptance is not overlooking the truth or denying reality. It is not the same thing as agreeing with or condoning. Nor does acceptance mean you never set limits. It does not mean you become a doormat or tolerate abusive behavior. Set limits, work issues, negotiate as needed, but with a kind and accepting heart.

Graceful Strategies

Let's consider the following strategies for acceptance:

- Don't overextend your reach.
- Become a vessel of grace.
- Defer to the Supreme Avenger.
- Look within.

Don't overextend your reach

We do not know the particulars of what triggered the accident that sent Grandfather plummeting. One theory is the roofer above Grandfather overextended his reach.

Author Gary Zukav demonstrated on *Oprah* how skilled roofers catch an object thrown to them when they are perched on a rooftop. They extend their arm, but will catch the object only if it is within arm's reach. If the toss falls short, they will not lean out and reach for it. They will let the object fall to the ground. Roofers know reaching too far leads to disaster. The length of their arm is the radius of their sphere of control.

We reach too far when we try to change other people instead of accepting them as they are. If I extend my arm and move it in a circle around my head, the circle surrounds the only person I have the ability to change: me. I have no power to change anyone else.

One of the most powerful ways to effect change is to change ourselves. Giving up the fight to control others frees us to determine our own response. The focus shifts from trying to change the other person to looking at self.

Become a vessel of grace

One of the best parts about the graceful life is realizing I am far from perfect, but God loves me anyway. Who am I to not extend the same privilege of imperfection to others? When I become a vessel for grace, I allow the gift of unmerited favor and forgiveness I receive to flow through me to others.

Other people have their own issues with which they are struggling. The less a person loves himself, the less love he will be able to offer you. How eloquently the New Testament teaches us to give grace anyway: "Finally, all of you, live in harmony with one another; be sympathetic, love as brothers, be compassionate and humble. Do not repay evil with evil or insult with insult, but with blessing, because to this you were called so that you may inherit a blessing."[74]

Do you see the word? *Harmony.* God wants us to "live in harmony."

We cannot experience peace by willpower alone, no matter how hard we try. We are made to seek God. Only by staying in relationship with Him and becoming a vessel of grace do we have any hope for living in harmony and accepting people as they are.

Defer to the Supreme Avenger

Do you know to whom *mine* and *I* refers in the following passage? "It is mine to avenge; I will repay. In due time their foot will slip; their day of disaster is near and their doom rushes upon them."[75]

If you haven't figured it out yet, read on. "The Lord will judge his people and have compassion on his servants when he sees their strength is gone and no one is left, slave or free."[76]

The Lord, the Supreme Avenger, is on call for justice.

Look within

Fear-based emotions keep us from loving and accepting others.

Our ability to accept others is closely tied to our own self-esteem. When we love ourselves, it is easier to accept people as they are. When we feel inferior, acceptance is difficult.

What bothers us about someone else is often the same quality we see in ourselves. We notice the flaw because we are so familiar with it. The advice we give to others might be what we need to hear. We might be embarrassed by a family member's weakness and view it as a negative reflection on ourselves.

Often, when we attempt to change another person, we are expecting him or her to fill a void within us. We look to others to validate us or make us happy. Only by developing a relationship with God will we be able to satisfy the deepest longings of our heart.

Consider the following questions when you are struggling to accept another person.[77]

- Am I seeking validation or happiness from another person instead of accepting love from God?

- What about *me* is inhibiting acceptance?

- Do I have the quality I am viewing as a flaw in someone else?

- Am I struggling with self-love?

- Am I struggling for control?

- Am I struggling to belong?

- Is my motive self-seeking?

- Do I want the other person to change to help me look or feel better?

- Have I acknowledged that the other person has his own issues? Am I allowing grace to flow through me anyway?

- Do I seek peace or do I want to mold the perfect person?

CHAPTER FOUR

Living with Meaning

Have you ever asked yourself any of the questions below? If so, you, like many people, have been challenged to understand how you can live with a sense of meaning and purpose.

- Why am I here?

- Is this all there is?

- What is my purpose in life?

- How can I experience passion?

- What is the meaning of life?

Survival Through Meaning

Author Victor Frankl got his challenge in a Nazi concentration camp and later wrote about it in *Man's Search For Meaning*. Frankl survived the brutality that took the lives of his mother, father, brother, and wife. He lost everything he owned.

Frankl hid the manuscript for a book he was writing in his coat, but his captors seized it when he entered the Auschwitz concentration camp. Without much hope for survival, Frankl began to despair. His book would never come to be if he did not survive and rewrite it. Frankl believes his determination to rewrite his book gave his life meaning and helped him survive the fierceness of the concentration camps.[78]

Meaning enters our lives through our relationships and by living in accordance with God's plan. You do not "find" your purpose through goal setting and achievement, although proper planning and preparation are important. Your purpose unfolds as you seek to understand God's desires for you and trust Him to help you follow His will.

You were born with talents, given to you as a gift of grace, to be used in a way to help others. Passion, purpose, and meaning are the by-product of living in accordance with the divine plan for your life. In *The Road Less Traveled,* Scott Peck wrote, "Once we perceive the reality of grace, our understanding of ourselves as meaningless and insignificant is shattered."[79]

We'll explore living with meaning further as we discuss:

- Passion

- Making a Difference

- Freedom from Illusions

- Dreams Come True

- Joy in the Journey

- Foot Washing for Grace

Passion

Trapped underneath a raft, whirling among the rapids, was not where I planned to be when I geared up for a day of rafting. It was mid-June and the river was running high. Dave and I were floating with a group of friends in the most treacherous stretch of whitewater in the Snake River outside of Jackson Hole, Wyoming. Professional photographers climbed down the precipitous mountain slope to the water's edge, hoping the rafters would survive the whitewater and purchase their photos at the end of the trip.

I had chosen my raft carefully: big. The oarsman was a good friend who rafted professionally and had never flipped a boat.

We entered the rapids with momentum and hit the waves head-on. To survive, all we passengers had to do was hold on; surely, the raft would not flip end to end.

Our rubber roller coaster journeyed up and down over the swells. We wedged our toes between the rubber tube and the floor of the raft to anchor ourselves for the jarring ride.

Rapids crashed above our heads. My hands seized the aluminum tube on top of the raft.

Waves engulfed the boat. I tightened my grip.

Up and up we went. My fingernails dug into the palms of my hands, until up, up, and . . . over. Thunderous waves flipped our raft, end to end, even though we knocked into them squarely and with plenty of speed.

All six of us were thrown beneath the raft and trapped underwater in the churning, forty-three-degree whitewater.

Whether you can swim or not makes little difference at that point. You go where the river torrents hurl you.

The flailing arms and legs of the other rafters struck me as we struggled underneath the raft. Oddly, I found this comforting because it meant I was not alone.

Clinging to Our Rafts

What is your raft? Is there something you are clinging to as the waves crash upon your head? Are you hanging on to an unhealthy relationship because you are afraid to be alone? Are you settling for a job you hate because it pays well? Do you face daily boredom because you are afraid to leave the security of your comfort zone?

My fellow rafters and I feared leaving the comfort and security of our raft so much that we found ourselves trapped underwater. We felt safe right up until it flipped.

The fear of leaving our comfort zone keeps us from living our passion. Venturing away from the raft is risky.

Author C. S. Lewis said, "You cannot go on being a good egg forever. You must either hatch or rot."[80]

Before Jeff Bezos founded Amazon.com, he created what he calls a "regret minimization framework." He pictured himself as an eighty-year-old man looking back on his life with as few regrets as possible.[81]

Bezos wanted to capitalize on the expanding Internet market in a way that would make people's lives easier. Selling books seemed to be a good opportunity. Bezos evaluated the idea. He reasoned he would not regret trying and failing, but would regret never having tried. Bezos left his job on Wall Street to follow his dream. Amazon.com was born. Bezos started work in his garage on a $300,000 loan from his parents. He packed books on his hands and knees on a hard, concrete floor. He wrote the business plan in the car on a trip across the country while his wife drove.

Today, Bezos is up off the floor and no longer packs the books. Amazon.com grew to four thousand employees in four years. Bezos has amassed a fortune estimated to be worth billions of dollars.

All because he left the security of his raft to pursue his passion.

Life-Giving Benefits

Bill Gates is the richest man in the world, according to some calculations. His fortune has been estimated to be as high as $73 billion. He and his wife established a foundation that gave away $17 billion at one time—in a check with nine zeros. Gates has publicly stated he will give away most of his fortune during his lifetime. He feels passing on large amounts of wealth to his children is not in their best interest. He does not want to diminish their desire to be productive. Gates claims his daily work routine hasn't changed much since acquiring his fortune.

Have you ever wondered why people like Jeff Bezos and Bill Gates keep working when they could afford to quit? They are passionate about their work.

The line between work and play is blurred when you pursue your passion. A job does not feel like work when you love it. It's fun. At the end of the week you may even feel a twinge of sorrow because the workweek is over.

Pursuing your passion is exhilarating. It transports you into a new and exciting world.

Passion is energizing. When we say people are full of life, it means they have a zeal for life. Apathy drains life.

Thomas Jefferson died on July 4, 1826, exactly fifty years after he signed the Declaration of Independence. Jefferson spoke his last words on the evening of July 3, "Is it July fourth yet?"[82] He wasn't going anywhere until he celebrated the fiftieth anniversary of his passion.

Composer Ludwig van Beethoven said, shortly before he died in 1827, "I close my eyes with the blessed consciousness I have left one shining track upon the earth."

Graceful Strategies

Let's consider the following strategies for living with passion:

- Unveil your graceful gifts.

- Surrender to the divine plan.

- Plan and prepare.

Unveil your graceful gifts

When a daffodil bulb is planted, the bulb's mission is to produce a daffodil, not a tulip. If the bulb devoted its energy to trying to become a tulip, it would never succeed. Nor would it realize its natural beauty as a daffodil.

You were born with incredible gifts. The book of Romans teaches, "We have different gifts, according to the grace given us."[83] These gifts are yours to contribute to humanity.

Here's the best part. Whatever your special gifts are, you love to use them! When you are doing what you are born to do, you experience a deep sense of joy, fulfillment, and meaning.

Are you a daffodil or a tulip? Are you called to enforce the law or teach the law? Are you a visionary of the big picture or are you a master at carrying out the details? One mother opened a health food store after she saved her child's life with

a unique diet and vitamin therapy. A woman with a passion for music made it her mission to teach piano and voice to inner-city children. A friend who has always loved arts and crafts turned her passion into a "hobby that pays." Two women who liked to shop developed a multimillion-dollar business shopping and preparing gift baskets for movie stars such as Julia Roberts, George Clooney, Eddie Murphy, and Elton John.
What are your gifts?
How can you use them to help others?

Surrender to the divine plan

After our raft flipped, I thrashed about underneath it. I pushed upward for air, but crashed into the raft. The whitewater spun me back down. I wrestled toward the surface. Again, the raft was a barricade between the sky and me. I wished I had filled my lungs with air before landing in the water. I tussled. The water churned.

Finally, I popped out from underneath the raft. Oxygen! I could breathe.

Finding your passion is like breathing. You *want* to do it. You *have* to do it.

People have commented about how disciplined I must be to write a book. True, writing requires discipline, but love motivates me more than discipline. This book was inside of me. It has been a joy letting it out. Why wouldn't I want to do something I love?

Risk is one reason we can be reticent. Discovering passion requires us to risk leaving the security of our comfort zone. If I had not chosen to leave a lucrative twenty-year career in computer software engineering, my dream would be burning within me.

My fellow rafters and I landed underneath the raft because we did not want to leave the security of it. But what we viewed as our security was not so safe after all. We would have been better off letting go of the raft so we did not end up trapped underwater. Instead, the thing we clung to was our nemesis.

The only real security is in God.

Finding purpose is about surrendering, not searching, and using the gifts given to you. Living God's plan is how a daffodil bulb grows into a daffodil and not a tulip. "For I know the plans I have for you," declares the Lord, "plans to prosper you and not to harm you, plans to give you hope and a future."[84]

I mentioned the flailing arms and legs of the other people underneath the raft reassured me because it meant I was not alone. If people trapped under a raft, struggling for air, calmed me, imagine my comfort level if I would only remember the Supreme Comforter is always with me.

The old Proverb teaches us to, "Trust in the Lord with all thine heart; and lean not unto thine own understanding. In all thy ways acknowledge Him, and He shall direct thy paths."[85] This is the how-to of finding your passion.

Develop a relationship with God, surrender, and trust. Through a relationship with God, the Holy Spirit will guide you to your passion and help you understand God's plan for your life. By surrendering, you allow God to "direct your paths." By trusting, you receive the courage to leave the security of your comfort zone and live in accordance with God's plan for your life.

God will give you the grace you need to live in accordance with His plans for you. And you will be richly rewarded as you live passionately with a sense of meaning and purpose.

Plan and prepare

Opportunity is lost without planning and preparation. If I am going in for surgery, I prefer the person holding the knife to be someone who is trained in surgery. It goes without saying it takes time to plan and prepare for your life's mission.

Living with purpose does not mean you abdicate your responsibilities or abandon your family in pursuit of passion. Priorities change over time, depending on family and personal needs. Life balance includes integrating passion and responsibilities as you love and serve the world around you.

Making a Difference

One group of rabbits thrived while the others languished in a study conducted by Ohio State University to determine the correlation between a high-cholesterol diet and heart disease. Researchers fed rabbits toxic diets and observed the effects. One group had significantly fewer symptoms than the others.

Puzzled, the researchers were at a loss to explain this variance.

Inadvertently, they discovered the researcher who fed the strongest group cuddled and held the rabbits before he fed them. Love and affection accounted for the difference.[86]

All researchers had the same task: feed the rabbits and observe the effects of the toxic diet. And yet, one researcher made a positive impact on the health and well-being of a group of rabbits. By cuddling them, he realized different results than those of his coworkers.

Making a Difference

Like the researcher cuddling rabbits, you can make an impact in the lives of those around you by infusing love into your daily work. Whatever the task, you can make it meaningful.

Work does not mean you are getting paid in a job outside your home. Raising young children and volunteering in your community is meaningful work. The key is you are engaged in productive activities and adding value to the world around you.

You have the opportunity to make a difference in the world every day.

The difference between a meaningful and meaningless job is often perception, or attitude. Living with a sense of significance can be as simple as changing your perspective. A determination to make an impact and to help others as you perform your daily duties may be all you need to enrich your life and the lives of those around you.

Ideally, your primary work coincides with your purpose in life since it is the place where you spend the majority of your day. Not everyone is fortunate enough to have their vocation match their passion. If this is the case and you are unable to leave your current work, long-range planning will help you reach your goal and you can supplement your primary work with volunteer service in the interim.

Meaningless Consequences

As we scramble from task to task, many of us long for more leisure time. The reality is most of us need more rest, but not more leisure. The human brain wants to be stimulated. The heart wants to serve.

Holocaust survivor Victor Frankl watched fellow prisoners die shortly after losing their sense of purpose. Most people do not die a physical death, but many die spiritually. They lose their zeal, their passion for life. Days are long and unfulfilling. Apathy, frustration, boredom, fear, feeling incapable, envy, and depression are some of the consequences of living without a sense of meaning.

Graceful Strategies

Let's consider the following strategies for making a difference:

- Understand the mission.

- Be creative.

- Minister.

Understand the mission

Understand how the work being performed contributes to humanity. This involves seeing past the immediate task. A mother sees above the pile of dirty laundry to her angel in diapers. A teacher sees past Tuesday's math assignment and remembers she is helping to shape the next generation. A bus driver caught among honking horns in traffic understands mass transit is important for a healthier environment and knows he is helping those unable to afford a car. The garbage collector remembers when the city of New York was paralyzed without his services.

Be creative

We have all done business with clerks who go out of their way to serve. Others seem irritable and reluctant to help. Many white-collar workers are professional meeting-goers who prefer to leave the creativity and productivity to someone else.

You have likely heard the expression twenty percent of the people do eighty percent of the work. The "twenty-percenters" also tend to feel a greater sense of satisfaction—adding value, being creative, and producing reaps fulfillment.

Minister

Preachers are not the only people who are called to minister. We all are.

Mother Teresa did not stride onto the world stage as the saint she later became. She stepped into one small corner of a broken world and held the hand of an ailing person. After caring for that person, she moved on to the next.

"It is not what we do but how much love we put into it," Mother Teresa said. She told some people who went to help in Calcutta to find their own Calcutta. You don't need to move to the slums of India to make a difference. Find your own small corner of the world and minister.

You are surrounded daily by broken spirits. Those who are not shattered are so fragile they need daily doses of love.

You can make a difference. The opportunity is present for everyone, whether you are a carpool driver, a CEO, a member of the PTA, or working in a nine-to-five job. The type of work does not matter. How you pursue it makes the difference.

Our egos want us to believe if we let our guard down, especially in the workplace, and become more caring we might lose in the competitive world. But the effort will not go unnoticed.

Freedom from Illusions

A farmer thought he had seen an army of ghosts while digging wells outside of Xian, China, in 1974. He trembled as he sprinted out of the ground. Sixteen feet beneath the surface of the earth, he had discovered the Terracotta Warriors, buried two thousand years before. Terracotta comes from the root words *terra,* meaning clay and *cotta,* meaning baked. The farmer had unearthed an army of baked clay.

Two thousand years later, on a trip to China, I watched workers meticulously unearth new clay figures still being discovered. Gardening tools chipped the dirt away that surrounded the outside of the figures. Small brushes dusted dirt from the soldiers' faces.

The emperor of an ancient dynasty commissioned the Terracotta Warriors and an underground tomb to keep evil spirits away and protect his soul in the after life. Seven thousand life-sized soldiers, horses, and chariots are housed in an underground palace. Each warrior has a different expression. Each was given an authentic weapon. All face east in the direction of the emperor's enemies. Some are archers; others are soldiers, generals, or officers. A power structure exists even in clay armies.

What the emperor really wanted was for seven to eight thousand people to be buried alive with him. But his inner circle advised him the peasants might not appreciate being buried alive. Three hundred thousand peasants were already off building the Great Wall of China. To bury thousands more alive might incite a revolt, the emperor's advisors cautioned.

The emperor reconsidered. He enlisted the help of seven hundred thousand peasants to build the underground palace and imperial army of baked clay. Construction took thirty-eight years and was not completed at the time of the emperor's death. His son completed the task.

Material World

It's difficult to understand the logic of a man so powerful and wealthy he created an underground palace in the hope of eternal rest after death. Most people in modern-day society understand the emperor's hopes were an illusion.

But our egos create illusions we don't recognize. Our egos coax us to project a certain type of image and chase money, power, status, and achievement. Our egos entice us to strive to be the best, achieve more, accumulate wealth and possessions, and receive the next promotion even if it's in a job we hate.

But prizes of the ego can be a burden.

A material approach enslaves us to things and achievements. Money, power, status, and achievement are seductive, but they will never fill a spiritual void. Proverbs teaches, "A pretentious, showy life is an empty life; a plain and simple life is a full life."[87] Nothing is inherently wrong with buying nice things. I would rather have money than not any day. The problem is when we are driven by external rewards at the expense of spiritual ones.

Americans living in the present day should be the happiest people who ever lived if money buys happiness. Nowhere else in the world, and at no other time in the history of man, have people had more than Americans do today. Why, then, are so many people unhappy?

The only people who believe money cannot buy happiness are the wealthy.

At the top of her career, singer Celine Dion performed a farewell concert and returned home—a place she and her husband had not spent two months together. She appeared to have it all, but Dion wanted out. And so she took a two-year break.

Dion's fame amassed her a fortune most people only dream about. She traveled the world, rode in chauffeur-driven limousines, wore expensive clothes, and stayed in the best hotels. A staff of people took care of her every need. Not only did room service bring her breakfast each morning, someone ordered room service for her.

But Dion said she was ready to be "a normal person," "ready to cook," "drive [her] own car," and "pick [her] own tomatoes."

Non-Material Benefits

Meaning is not material. Meaning enters our lives through our relationships and by living into God's plan by using the gifts given to us, in grace, to love and serve humanity.

In moments when you allow yourself to be drawn into grace, you are freed from the burden of the ego's illusions. Life is enriched with meaning, joy, and passion. Your relationships improve. Gratitude for what you have replaces an insatiable longing for what you do not have. Serenity replaces a continual striving for more. Work energizes rather than drains you. Creativity soars.

Graceful Strategies

Let's consider the following strategies for living free from illusions:

- Move from having to being.

- Simplify.

Move from having to being

We cannot experience the fullness of life through achievement. Buying, searching, and striving keep us from life in the spirit.

In *To Have or to Be,* therapist Erich Fromm wrote that we have two basic states: having and being. *Being* is the experience of "inner activity" when we stop chasing material gains and empty ourselves for love. *Having* is describable in terms of things such as possessions, money, and jobs.

He cites examples of related teachings. The Buddha taught longing for material things will keep you from reaching nirvana. Mystic Meister Eckhart taught, to become more spiritual, we must transcend the ego. Karl Marx, coauthor of the *Communist Manifesto,* taught affluence could be as troublesome as poverty.[88]

Meister Eckhart said "blessed are the poor in spirit" speaks of an inner poverty when we do not want, know, or have anything. Not wanting means we no longer experience greed or envy. Not knowing is letting go of self-righteousness and the need to prove we are right. Not having is not being attached to material possessions, status, achievement, and work.[89]

Being penetrates the mask through a personal relationship with God and by accepting and giving grace. Only then can you experience the fullness of life.

Simplify

The concept of simplicity is simple. Simplicity is freedom from the bondage of things that are burdensome: compulsion for material goods, power, status, money, and achievement. It is a retreat from a hectic pace keeping us so busy we don't have time for that which is most important. Less becomes more.

Simplicity begins with the understanding that wealth and the good life are lived in the spirit, not through the material world. It is acknowledging that every blessing is a gift of grace.

Dreams Come True

Imagine racing on a bicycle in the Tour de France, more 2,500 miles for three weeks—from New York City to Seattle, or from Los Angeles to Washington, D.C. Now picture yourself spinning that distance up mountain passes so steep some cars strain up them. Two hundred athletes compete for the Tour's coveted yellow jersey.

The competitors bike up to 150 miles a day. Their hearts pound 180 beats per minute. They climb the Alps and Pyrenees mountains, cross the flats of central France, and tour neighboring countries. They zip through picturesque mountain towns along narrow roads lined with cheering fans. They jet down winding mountain roads at speeds of more than sixty miles per hour.

At the completion of the Tour de France, the party of all cycling parties follows in Paris. Well-wishers raise glasses filled with bubbly to toast the festivities. When the participants' hearts pound at this party, it is because their dreams have come true.

After being given a forty percent chance of living, Lance Armstrong triumphed four times in the Tour de France. His are victories of the human heart. Testicular cancer had spread throughout Armstrong's body to his abdomen, lungs, and brain. Armstrong had surgery to remove the cancer ravaging his body. Throughout 1996 and 1997 he endured chemotherapy so strong it caused internal burns.

Barbara Walters selected Armstrong for her *Most Fascinating Person of 1999* television special. He was chosen as one of *People* magazine's most intriguing people.

Fueled by a fierce determination, Armstrong engaged in a rigorous training program. Through perseverance and a healthy dose of divine intervention, Armstrong's dream came true.

Passion, Purpose, and Courage

Life is an exciting adventure when you live with passion and a sense of purpose. Your passion and dreams align with the divine plan for your life.

Following your dream takes courage. Courage is misunderstood. Some people equate it with being fearless. But courageous people fear. They face difficult situations in spite of their fears.

Eleanor Roosevelt said, "You gain strength, courage, and confidence by every experience in which you really stop to look fear in the face. . . . You must do the thing you think you cannot do."[90]

Different Parts, Equal Value

No one prevails in the Tour de France without his team. Nine athletes are on each of the twenty-one competing teams. The teammates' job is to help the lead biker cross the finish line first.

Lance Armstrong graciously acknowledges the role his team plays in victory. The team brings Armstrong water when he is thirsty, feeds him when he is hungry, and shields him from the wind by riding at the front of the pack while Armstrong rides closely behind the team to save his energy. Near the finish line, the team moves aside. Armstrong breaks free to cross the line in victory.

The team is in the backdrop. I cannot tell you the name of one person on Armstrong's team. But the world knows the name Lance Armstrong.

The team makes the Tour possible. Imagine pedaling for 2,500 miles, your heart pounding so hard you feel nauseous, to help another guy cross the finish line first. Nine guys were on the U.S. team, but only one could finish first. The others served in the shadows of the winner's spotlight. Every teammate was critically important. The eight who followed are of equal value to the one who led. Without the team, there would be no Tour.

You were created to live with purpose and to pursue your part on the team. Each part is a different role, all of equal value.

Graceful Strategies

Let's consider the following strategies for living your dreams:

- Embrace the uncertainty of the graceful path.

- Believe.

Embrace the uncertainty of the graceful path

Passion is experienced through the unknown.

Prior to his illness, Armstrong had not considered competing in one of the most difficult athletic events in the world. Armstrong explains his illness "reset all expectations . . . to zero." Unencumbered by expectations, Armstrong was free to pursue his dream, reasoning he had "nothing to lose." His message for others, "there's hope."[91]

With every pump of the pedal, Armstrong rode down an uncertain path and on to his dream.

Living with passion often brings you face to face with the uncertainty of new experiences. Uncertainty is not the same thing as impossibility. Taking on a challenge with an unknown outcome such as a new project, changing jobs, making new friends, traveling, or learning a new skill can be invigorating. Following your dream is exhilarating. Situations you are anxious about are often also exciting. Part of accepting the uncertainty of the graceful path is to embrace the excitement of the unknown.

Believe

Lonnie Johnson's dream was born in his bathroom. Johnson liked to tinker. As a child, he built a robot and won the state science fair.

Johnson wanted to become an engineer; some people advised him to become a technician instead. But he focused on his goals and pursued his dream. He received his master's degree in nuclear engineering and began work as an engineer at NASA. In his free time, he tinkered.

Johnson experimented with a nozzle in his bathroom and noticed the curtains sway. The stream of water from the nozzle created a forceful turbulence and air currents. He dreamed about a great water gun and later developed the Super Soaker. Today, over two hundred and fifty million Super Soakers have been sold.[92]

Nestled in the vast wilderness of Arizona, is a small Indian village. It sits among sheer red rock walls near the banks of blue-green waterfalls. Access to the village is either on foot or by mule. The route is impassible by automobile. Mules deliver supplies and mail.

My family and I stumbled upon the village after hiking on foot for eight miles on a backpacking trip one summer. The residents did not have cars, televisions, or phones. But in the isolation of the quaint, picturesque village, two young Indian boys played with Super Soakers!

All because Johnson believed in his dream.

Belief is the cornerstone of realized dreams. For people who live their dreams, problems and shortcomings are challenges, not excuses for quitting. Believing includes surrendering by accepting God's will, having the faith to pursue the divine plan for your life, and trusting that God will be with you as you do.

God-confidence creates self-confidence. If you pursue your calling, and if it is God's plan for you, *it* will happen. *It* does not mean winning the Tour de France or selling 250 million Super Soakers. *It* means living the life you were created to live. With perseverance and by putting your hand in God's, you will experience contentment as your dreams come true.

Joy in the Journey

Lucky for me, Dad is a gentleman. Otherwise, I might have never been born. Let me explain.

In his days of playing football and jumping hurdles, Dad's friends invited him to a party. Dad did not have a date, but he had friends who thought he should, so they found a date for him.

His friends made all the arrangements, with everyone in the know except Dad.

When his friends unveiled their plans, Dad said that sounded great except for one thing. He was not going on a blind date. With their heads hung low and eyes fixed upon the floor, his matchmaker friends confessed. Everything was set up, including the young lady who was expecting him.

This is when Dad's gentlemanly trait emerged. Dad was too gracious to back out, because he knew to do so would leave an unassuming young lady on a blind date without her date. And so, he went.

Any hesitation Dad might have had dissipated the moment the spotlight shone and took *blind* out of the words *blind date.* Stars glistened. The symphony played. Dad had chanced upon a real babe. And the babe discovered quite the hunk.

Two weeks of dating, a year of letter writing when Dad sailed the South Pacific with the Navy, followed by a weeklong reunion, and down the aisle they strolled. Dad and Mom became partners for life.

Blessings of "Un"

Who could have predicted the outcome of that momentous blind date? Who knew a fifty-eight-year and counting joyful journey was in the making?

Some of life's greatest blessings are described with "un" adjectives. Unanticipated blessing. Unplanned good fortune. Unexpected gain. Unsolicited advantage. Unscheduled windfall. Unpredicted benefit. Unforeseen treasure.

The problem is we can become so focused on the outcome we miss the journey. Priorities get out of balance. External factors motivate us rather than our internal value system as we seek artificial rewards. When we become fixated on a particular path, we often miss the better way.

How do you live in the present and enjoy the journey instead of being so driven toward a particular outcome? The secret lies in learning to trust in some different "un" words: uncertainty, unknown, unattached.

In the graceful life, you open yourself to risk the unknown, embrace uncertainty, and trust in the outcome by living into the divine plan for your life. You remain passionate and committed to the process, but unattached to a particular outcome.

Your calling is often found amid uncertainty. As you make choices to align your will with divine will, you will experience a joyful journey rich in blessings more extravagant than you can imagine.

All because of one other "un" word: unfailing love.

Graceful Strategies

Let's consider the following strategies for living with joy in the journey:

- Watch for providential paths.

• Focus on the journey, not the outcome.

Watch for providential paths

She could have missed it. Most people would have. But not her. Her résumé includes thirty-five Emmy Awards, the highest-rated talk show in television history, a book club that created instant bestsellers, *Newsweek*'s "Woman of the Century" (January 2001), one of *Time* magazine's 100 most influential people of the twentieth century (June 1998), Academy Award nominee, and a magazine named after the first letter of her first name—a single letter of the alphabet identifies her.

In the early days of her career, and against the advice of some friends, she quit her job coanchoring the six o'clock news in Baltimore. She embraced uncertainty and moved to Chicago in 1984 to host the local talk show *A.M. Chicago*. Two years later, the show became nationally syndicated and number one in the ratings.[93]

You know the show that bears her name: *Oprah.*

Lucky break or providential blessing?

An adopted baby girl became a nurse when she grew up. She began work in the local hospital and was assigned to care for an older woman, while working alongside of another nurse. After becoming acquainted with the others, she made an alarming discovery. The patient was her biological grandmother. The other nurse was her biological sister.

Coincidence or divine incident?

An artist was heartbroken when her work was not selected for display at a prestigious art gallery in another state. Feeling rejected and depressed, she returned home. The following year she sold more than a million dollars worth of artwork in her home state.

131

Personal windfall or divine planning?

The family of a dying man is told he will not survive the night. The man makes a miraculous recovery. The medical community called it a spontaneous growth cure.

Medical miracle or divine intervention?

In *Addiction and Grace,* Gerald May wrote, "Miracles are nothing other than God's ordinary truth seen through surprised eyes."[94]

God is always at work. The Spirit blows us like the wind. We never know which way the hand of God will lead us, only that the hand is always there.[95]

As you allow yourself to be drawn into grace, you open yourself to exploring the providential paths of divine planning.

Dad journeyed down a providential path, and the Spirit blew in Mom. Then came four unforeseen treasures: my wonderful sister, two fantastic brothers, and with humble boldness I include one other: me.

That is why I am grateful Dad is a gentleman.

Focus on the journey, not the outcome

Olympic swimmer Jeff Rouse was born to swim. He started at age five and swam his way into the Olympics.

As the world record holder in the hundred-meter backstroke, Rouse was favored to win in the 1992 Barcelona Olympics. He won a gold medal in the relay, but the prize for his individual event was silver, which is incredible, but Rouse sought gold. The quest for gold is something only an Olympic athlete can fully understand. Rouse committed to an arduous four-year training program to take one step higher on the podium in Atlanta in 1996.

The non-physical aspect of Rouse's approach is interesting. He incorporated spirit into his training program.

Rouse hired a sports psychologist who explained a fierce determination to win could keep a person from victory. Note the emphasis—to *win*. No one achieves Olympic gold without a zealous determination. Only through intense training can one qualify to compete with the world's best in a particular sport. The predicament is becoming so focused on the outcome that it inhibits your ability to win.

Rouse's love of swimming became an important aspect of his training program.

His walk to the starting blocks four years later in Atlanta was different. He found his family in the stands. In 1992 success meant winning. In 1996, he had come to terms with the possibility of not winning. Rouse's emphasis was on the middle of the race, not the outcome.

The result? His dream came true. He ascended one step higher on the podium. By reclaiming joy in the journey and relinquishing control of the outcome, Rouse won a gold medal.

Isn't that something? Spirit counts even when training for the Olympics.

Outcome-oriented goals categorize results into win/lose dichotomies. Goals are useful to the extent they provide a plan for moving in a certain direction. The problem is when emotional energy and feelings of self-worth are tied to a specific result over which you have no control. Jeff Rouse's worth was not tied to the outcome of his Olympic race for gold.

To paraphrase the popular expression "success is a journey, not a destination," focus on the journey, not the outcome. The joy is in the journey, not the achievement.

This means, in school, the focus is on learning rather than grades. At work, the emphasis is on doing a quality job, enjoying your work, and being kind to your coworkers rather than the next promotion. Driving includes enjoying the scenery along the way. Parents' emphasis is on loving their children and spending time together instead of raising the best athlete or the class valedictorian.

Life is a growth-process. Nobody masters life. Fulfillment is not in the outcome. Fulfillment is in the living, moment to moment. Yes, plan and prepare, but who knows what curves the future will bring?

The outcome of the Olympics was out of Rouse's control. If he focused on it, he would be trying to control circumstances beyond his control. Lots of things could have kept him from gold. The only real power Rouse had after diving off the starting block was the result of choices he made in the present moment. He could choose his attitude and actions, but was powerless over the outcome.

The outcome is out of our control, so why focus on it?

Was Dad focused on the outcome of his blind date? No. Did he even dream his friends' scheming would lead to wedded bliss? Certainly not, but it did.

And so I suggest, as someone who is the product of an unexpected result, focus on the journey, not the outcome. Travel down providential paths. Experience the joy in the journey.

Foot Washing for Grace

The world stands in awe of a small but powerful woman. She wore no makeup and dressed in sandals and a sari. Her image was different than the airbrushed models on the covers of women's magazines. She did not live in a mansion on the hill. Her home was in the slums.

Mother Teresa devoted her life to serving the poor on the streets of Calcutta. She was living proof of the power of love. Her life was service in action and as close as humans get to agape—perfect, other-centered love. She was selflessly devoted to the welfare of others.

India honored her with a funeral of the state, even though she was a Christian in a Hindu country. Agape love spans religious boundaries.

Riches to Rags to Blessings

A friend's brother was a prosperous physician when he met Mother Teresa. His life has never been the same. Leaving his medical practice and material possessions behind, he moved to Calcutta to serve beside her.

His riches-to-rags story has a fairy-tale ending. This doctor-turned-priest, who traded material wealth for a life of service on the streets in Calcutta, has been blessed with a tremendous sense of peace.

We have been created with such magnificence that when we spotlight grace by serving others, the light bounces back to us. When we serve others, our own lives are enriched.

Psychologist Abraham Maslow performed a study of happy people. He found when a person is "radiantly alive," he is living for a purpose "beyond himself."

Winston Churchill said, "We make a living by what we get. We make a life by what we give." To live with passion is to live with a sense of purpose by loving and serving the world around you.

Service is love in action. Every act of service, no matter how small, puts more love into the world. Mother Teresa defined love as "giving until it hurts."[96]

Service is any act of kindness that is performed in the best interest of another person. This does not mean you do everything for another person. For example, it is often more appropriate for parents to train their children so they learn how to carry their own load. If parents carry their children's burdens for them, their help can hurt.

Dirty Feet Scrubbed Clean

Washing a guest's feet was an act of hospitality in Biblical times. During the Passover Feast, Jesus picked up a towel, filled a bowl with water, and washed the feet of his disciples—even Judas.[97] The same hands that would have nails driven through them washed the feet of the one who was to betray him.

Graceful Strategies

Let's consider the following strategies for graceful service:

- Humility is an integral part of service.

- Most acts of service are simple acts of kindness.

- Service is other-centered, not self-serving.

Humility is an integral part of service

When I think of washing someone else's feet today, one word comes to mind: *yuck*. When I think about washing the feet of a person in Biblical times two words come to mind: *double yuck*. They walked around barefoot, or in sandals at best. Bathing was done infrequently in the local river, and without soap.

Only the slaves performed such a mundane and disagreeable task such as washing another person's feet. And yet Jesus humbled himself in an act of total submission to teach the lesson of humility in service.

Most acts of service are simple acts of kindness

You do not need to give up your house and live on the streets of Calcutta to serve. Most acts of service are not the extraordinary tasks we make them out to be. What is more menial than washing someone's grimy feet?

The director of the local food bank told me most of their food donations come from people in less affluent neighborhoods. The poor know what it is like to be hungry. Perhaps that explains part of the reason caring people of affluence can be reluctant to serve. They do not understand the difference a can of soup can make.

Mother Teresa taught we love "not in big things, but in small things with great love."[98]

Author Leo Tolstoy passed a beggar on the street one day. Tolstoy dug into his pockets to find some change to give, but his pockets were empty. He apologized to the beggar saying, "I'm sorry, my brother, I have nothing to give."

The beggar replied, "You have given me more than I asked for. You have called me brother."[99]

As his son lay dying, a father remembered a couple from Stephen Ministries who came to the hospital. They didn't talk much. They sat. Twenty years later, the father remembered the profound impact these people made as they sat with him and shared his burden.

Service is anything that creates unity. To serve is to share some soup, aid the ailing, hammer nails for the homeless, invite the ignored, and give grace to the grouch. Many acts of service cost nothing and take little time: encouragement, compliments, listening, gratitude, and compassion. Anytime you affirm the worth of others, you serve.

Service is other-centered, not self-serving

Pamela Atkinson is an American Mother Teresa who serves in the obscurity of homeless camps. Before she retired, Atkinson spent her days as a corporate executive and evenings helping the homeless. Today, she is available to help fulltime. She has met with the governor of Utah dressed in blue jeans on her way to feed the hungry and clothe the needy. Because dogs are the only companions for many, she brings food for their dogs.

These are the people many of us look away from when we meet them on the street. Not Atkinson. She refers to them as her friends.

At the soup kitchen, Atkinson stands at the front of the line and shakes hands with hundreds of people who will be fed that night. One man looked at her with tears in his eyes as she took his hand; it was the first time someone had touched him in more than a year. Soup is for their stomachs. Handshakes feed their souls.

Atkinson developed tennis elbow from shaking hands. Her doctor advised her to stop, but she explained her mission is bigger than tennis elbow. Today she wears a bandage on her elbow and is still shaking hands.

Atkinson gives all the glory to God, explaining she could never do it on her own.

Jesus washed the disciples' feet in the anonymity of an upper room. No audience. No fans. Just some grimy feet and a washbowl. Only the men, whose feet he knelt before, were present. Jesus received no adulation from a crowd, no personal glorification.

He taught by example: Perform menial tasks with humility and be other-centered, not self-serving.

CHAPTER FIVE

The Spiritual Journey

Hikers have been found dead from dehydration in the Grand Canyon with full water bottles at their side. While dying of thirst, they did not pick up their water bottles and drink.

Hiking in the Grand Canyon is deceptive. The tough part of the hike, the uphill, is at the end when you are tired. Hikers begin at the rim and descend into the canyon toward the Colorado River. Because it is downhill on the way in, it's easy to hike in farther than your ability to climb out.

The elements intensify the danger. Scorching summer heat soars, sometimes to 120 degrees on the canyon floor. The rim is high above sea level where the air is thin, making breathing more difficult.

Underestimating your need for water can be life threatening. Rapid dehydration occurs without enough fluids. You can become dehydrated without feeling thirsty.

Many of us are, unknowingly, dying of a different type of thirst. Not a physical thirst, but a spiritual one.

We are spiritual beings. When we deny our spirituality, we deny who we are. Spiritually, we die of thirst with a "full water bottle." But it doesn't need to be this way.

The Sanctuary Within

While visiting Tibet, I gazed up at an austere monastery high in the Himalayan Mountains. It soared above the valley floor and blended into the landscape on the side of a mountain.

The only way to reach the monastery was on foot. Tibetan monks scale the rugged mountainside through thin air, 14,000 feet above sea level, to experience the serenity it offers. Even the elderly monks ascend to practice meditation and solitude. They climb to the roof of the world to journey inward.

Spirituality is not just for monks. We all yearn for spiritual fulfillment, including people living normal lives raising children and going to work every day.

Drawing closer to God and becoming more spiritually centered helps you develop a reverence for life. Relationships improve. Worries lessen. Blessings are found in the mundane. Less becomes more. Strangers become friends.

When you nurture your spirituality, you journey to the sanctuary within, a place of inner retreat no one else can reach. You are freed to experience serenity among the chaos. This does not mean you never experience conflict, but when you do, inner tranquility helps you respond in grace.

Choosing the spiritual journey is a magnificent way to travel through a troubled world, living in the hope and safety of God's loving care.

Spirituality or Religion?

Terrorists turned airplanes into flying missiles and propelled them into the World Trade Center. Teenagers opened fire on their classmates in a high school cafeteria. A crazed gunman entered the sanctuary of a church and gunned down children during choir practice. No mother should have to hear the terror in her child's voice as he recounts the horror of hiding under a church pew to escape madness.

Laws cannot cure the broken spirits of such evil acts. The heart must be changed.

Your heart is transformed as you allow yourself to be immersed in grace and develop a personal relationship with God. This helps you develop an awareness that blessings are from God. This is a process. Moment by moment, you are free to choose to love God, accept God's love for you, and administer grace to others. Sacred moments are those in which you relinquish self-sufficiency, recognize your dependence on, and trust in God. Instead of knowing *about* God, you know Him. These are blessed moments.

Spirituality is not the same as religion. It is not synonymous with going to church or understanding religious doctrine. Some spiritual people never go to church. Others who spend a lot of time in the pew on Sunday spend little time in relationship with The One they come to worship. Personal relationship is the key.

We'll explore the spiritual journey as we discuss:

- Knowing God

- Centering Prayer

- Gratitude and Grace

- Solitude

Knowing God

"I love him so much." I read these words in a letter from a friend.

My friend is a cute, single gal.

Is she in love? I wondered. My first thought was she had started dating someone special.

I reread her words. Turns out she is in love, but not with Prince Charming. My friend has fallen deeply in love with God.

Searching for Fullness

Too often, as we seek love, we ignore the Greatest Love of all. Our yearning for God is so fundamental to our existence that, by design, the yearning is never completely satisfied. The longing keeps us seeking and growing.

One of the things He wants most is our friendship. It is difficult to appreciate the magnificence of something so vast you can never fully understand it. The sacred landscape is too overwhelming, too grand, and too incomprehensible. A personal relationship with God frees you to live in hope and reach through the brokenness with healing hands to a world desperately in need of grace.

It is then that you learn how to love and be loved and to live with meaning.

Self, Self, and More Self

He had escaped from his mother and was hanging from the monkey bars when I saw him. Life was good. This toddler was king of the playground. It's not often a child so young can assume top honors, but in his case it was easy. He was the only person on the playground.

I was volunteering at my daughter's school and noticed him as I passed by a window. Because he was alone, I seized him and brought him inside—much to his disappointment.

He was at the stage where kids waddle instead of walk. I picked him up, ostensibly to help him down the stairs, but the real reason was he was darling.

"No. I do it myself," he demanded.

I sighed and put him down.

"I do it myself. I do it myself. I do it myself." He repeated the words like a mantra all the way down the stairs.

Self-sufficiency starts young.

The I-do-it-myself syndrome keeps us from accepting the gift of God's grace. Can you relate to its symptoms? Do you:[100]

- Resort to self-mastery or surrender to the Master?

- Run on willpower or rest in the Greater Power?

- Strive for your will or accept divine will?

- Fear the future or trust in the Planner of the future?

- Seek control or seek the Kingdom?

- Walk alone or lean on God?

A Changed Heart

Imagine watching all the blood drain out of a person's body. My eyes fixed upon blood flowing through tubes as I gazed at patients undergoing artificial kidney dialysis. It was the hands-on part of a high school science project.

The kidneys clean the blood, filter toxic waste products, and help maintain healthy body chemistry. In other words, the kidneys filter out the bad stuff and maintain proper levels of the good stuff. A pair of bean-shaped organs about five inches long undertakes this.

Toxic wastes build up in the body when the kidneys fail. Artificial dialysis filters the blood the ailing kidneys cannot.

One type of dialysis draws the blood out of the body, pumps it through the filter of a machine, cleanses the blood, and sends it back into the body through a vein for new life.

Remarkable!

Kidneys cleanse the blood. The organ for spiritual cleansing is the heart. "Create in me a clean heart, O God," David penned in the Psalm.[101] "Above all else, guard your heart, for it is the wellspring of life," according to Solomon's proverb.[102]

A changed heart changes your life. While we have the responsibility to make good choices, it takes the power of grace to change our hearts. Legalistic approaches and trying harder are never enough without internal, spiritual transformation.

When a person's kidneys fail, the patient chooses whether or not to undergo dialysis. After that, the dialysis machine does the work.

On the spiritual journey, your choice is whether or not to accept the gift of grace and enter into a personal relationship with God. When you accept the invitation, God does the work of changing your heart. He transforms you from the inside out.[103]

Fear of punishment does not change a heart of hatred to one of love. Spiritual transformation does.

An unclean heart circulates misery, hatred, fear, and resentment. A transformed heart circulates grace.

Vessels of Grace

If someone were to ask me, "What is the primary thing I can do to improve my relationships, love myself, and live with meaning?" I would respond, "Know God. Receive and reflect grace." Six words summarize the central message of this book.

Let God fill you with His Spirit; you will then become a vessel of grace. The "Spirit of the Living God" is written "not on tablets of stone but on tablets of human hearts," the Apostle Paul said.[104]

The commandment to "love the Lord your God with all your heart and with all your soul and with all your strength" is not an edict.[105] It is an appeal to the heart. Inviting God into your life is a longing, not an obligation, a joy not a burden. It is the only way to quench the thirst, the only way to heal the ache. In the Old Testament, God explains the commandments are "for your own good."[106]

You are healed through the transforming love of God. As you are healed, the reverberating sounds of love begin to echo deep within, influencing your thoughts and actions.

In the words of Saint Augustine of Hippo, "Love God and do as you please."[107]

The self-sufficient try to propel themselves into goodness and happiness. But how good is good enough? If you focus on morality but neglect the importance of a personal relationship with God, you will never live in integrity. But when a relationship with God is maintained, morality follows.

Knowing Through Relationship

Western culture perpetuates the idea of an external God *out there* somewhere. The Bible teaches otherwise. "The kingdom of God is within you.[108] "The one who is in you is greater than the one who is in the world."[109]

This does not mean we are little gods. God works within, but is also separate and distinct from us. God is greater. God is always more.

The spiritual journey is the process of moving deeper into the kingdom of God. The quest to find one's self is really a journey to find God.

God provides refuge from the storm. Life's burdens do not seem so heavy. God does not make us immune to pain, but helps us endure it. He does not promise a life without struggles, but offers comfort and peace in spite of them. He is the source of strength to help you face your struggles. Our hunger for security, love, and belonging is fed through God, not the world. As we trust and believe, we begin to heal.

God created us to be in relationship with Him. This means knowing God through relationship rather than knowledge. It means resting in His presence and communicating with Him moment to moment, throughout the day. A friend explains, "Watch a child. He says, 'There is a God. I love God. God loves me. He and I are buddies.' He prays, 'Take care of my frog and my hamster. Bless Mommy and Daddy.' Accepting the Lord is the beginning. Then you move into friendship, working together daily. When you love God, God pours love into you."

You don't have to be a scholar of the holy texts to know God. He is not concerned with how much scripture you can quote or whether you went to church last Sunday, although worship and reading scripture are meaningful activities.

Legalism and works-oriented religion substitute rules, dogma, knowledge, and judgment at the expense of a personal relationship with God. It is not uncommon to become consumed with activities of religious institutional life and miss the joy, peace, and transformation of knowing God.

God asks two things of us: "love God" and "love your neighbor as yourself." Loving God is our only hope for loving our neighbors as ourselves.

We are wired to seek and must seek to find. "You will seek me and find me when you seek me with all your heart. I will be found by you," declares the Lord, "and will bring you back from captivity."[110] The promise is when we earnestly seek, we will find.

Head to Heart

On my own faith journey, I went through a period of intellectual inquiry, asking questions theologians have debated endlessly. Why do people suffer? Why do bad things happen to good people? Where was God during the Holocaust? Whose side is God on in war? Why does evil exist?

It was easy for me to see the hand of God when a terminally ill child was healed, but I was at a loss to explain the child who was not.

I am not much closer to being able to answer the tough questions today. Free will is part of the answer. We would not have free will if God controlled all of our actions. I also realize I am not capable of understanding the Master's plan. But I can rest in the assurance of God's plan if I can learn to trust in it.

Faith, by definition, involves trust without proof. Mystery and paradox are an integral part of faith. God is the ultimate mystery—perhaps by design, because it keeps us seeking Him.

In my journey into faith, I had been trying to solve the mystery and comprehend the unfathomable.

I now take comfort in knowing I don't have to solve the puzzle anymore than I have to understand how electricity works to know the lightbulb will light when I flip the switch. I can't explain the magnificence of creation either. But I marvel at the miracle of birth knowing it can only be an act of grace.

The mystery is not to be solved, but entered into.

Ultimately I have learned the path to faith is not through our heads, but through our hearts. This is not to suggest we no longer need to use our brain to ask questions. But we come to know God by experiencing God's presence.

I am humbled by the profound love of a deeply caring God whose infinite love is too vast to be understood by the limitations of my human mind.

Graceful Strategies

Let's consider the following strategies for knowing God:

- Ask, seek, and knock.

- Move deeper into friendship with God.

- Nurture your relationship.

Ask, seek, and knock

As Dave and I searched for Harvard one summer, Boston's one-way streets encircled us. We didn't know where we were going, but who needs a map? Dave has a knack for driving by feel. He calls it "the Karcher method."

The one-way streets usually headed in the opposite direction from the way we wanted to go. No left turn signs marked the intersections where we wanted to turn left. We veered right.

We swerved left. We crept down one-way streets the wrong way.

Our zigzag tactic was not working. We grabbed the map with a sigh, pulled over to the curb, and stopped.

As we unfolded the map, we glanced up. Directly in front of our car, a sign with an arrow read, "Harvard straight ahead."

The first step on the spiritual journey is to acknowledge our need for help. This is more than a casual request. It is a plea for mercy.

We did not find the sign leading us to Harvard until we surrendered and admitted defeat.

God often waits for us to seek His help before offering it. Oh, how our Mighty Friend loves it when we relinquish self-sufficiency and acknowledge we cannot do it alone.

Relinquish self-sufficiency, surrender, and trust.

"Ask and it will be given to you; seek and you will find; knock and the door will be opened to you."[111] At home. At work. When you are afraid. When you are tempted. When you are lonely.

Ask. Seek. Knock.

Move deeper into friendship with God

As we move deeper on the spiritual journey, our friendship with God becomes increasingly intimate. We move in and out of five stages of friendship at different times in our lives: stranger, acquaintance, casual friend, close friend, and soul mate. God is always available for the friendship, but we don't always accept the invitation.

- *Stranger:* You do not believe in or know God.

- *Acquaintance*: You know about God, but don't know Him. You would say you believe in God if asked.

- *Casual friend:* You visit with God occasionally, but not regularly. You may teach your kids to say prayers at meals and before bed, but your own personal prayers are sporadic. You believe in moral teachings and may work hard to fulfill religious obligations.

- *Close friend:* Your relationship with God is an important part of your life. You experience God's presence regularly.

- *Soul mate:* God is the center of your life. You have an intimate relationship with Him. You and God are steadfast companions, at one with each other. Theologians call this *union with God* or *resting in God.*

Nurture your relationship

Author Truman Capote said it once took him an entire day to write a single word, but it was the right word.

A friend who is a ski instructor spent an entire day learning the proper way to flick his wrist when he planted his ski pole in the snow.

An Olympic figure skater practices the same routine over and over for months, or even years, when training for a competition.

Growth takes time. Especially moving forward in your relationships.

For any relationship to thrive, it must be nurtured. Neglect it, for any reason—including busyness, no matter how virtuous— and the relationship suffers.

Relationship with God is no different.

If we don't replenish the well, it will run dry. Pray. Serve. Read and listen to inspirational material. Practice solitude. Observe the hand of God in everyday life. Visit with God anywhere and everywhere. And move deeper into relationship with Him.

Centering Prayer

News anchor Dan Rather asked Mother Teresa what she said when she prays.

"I listen," Mother Teresa replied.

"What does God say?" Rather continued.

"He listens," she answered.[112]

The temptation for many of us is to spend our prayer time doing a lot of talking, but not much listening. It's tough to hear God when we are speaking.

During centering prayer, God talks. You sit in silence and listen. Centering prayer helps you empty yourself of the noise of an external world and be filled with the presence of God.[113] When you are struggling with a problem, the deep inner-silence of centering prayer helps you hear the voice of God as He shines a lamp unto your feet and directs your path.

Hearing the Whisper

"Can you hear me?" the nurse asked Dave, during a hearing test for his first job after college.

"Yes," he replied.

She took five steps backward. "Can you hear me now?"

"Yes, again," Dave answered.

Her vocal cords controlled the volume. No fancy gadgets measured decibels during this hearing test. At five-step intervals—backwards—the nurse asked and Dave responded until . . . oops. She hit the wall at the end of the hall.

She turned the corner. With a barely audible voice she asked, "Can you hear me now?"

"Yes." Dave heard the whisper.

Centering prayer helps you hear the whispers of God. It brings you into a state of stillness and awakens you to God's presence, allowing you to hear the divine guidance reverberating within.

Author William McGill said, "The value of consistent prayer is not that He will hear us, but that we will hear Him."[114]

In the ongoing debate of quantity time versus quality time, quantity is key when it comes to prayer. What's important is not praying the perfect prayer, but that we pray. The real issue regarding prayer is not whether prayer should be taken out of public schools, but whether it has been taken out of our hearts.

Prayer is the primary means for establishing a relationship with God. Our connection moves past God of the foxhole to friend. We experience God through our hearts rather than relying solely on knowledge and doctrine.

Tranquil Waters

Have you ever snorkeled? My family loves guided snorkeling excursions.

"Touching coral kills it. It grows at a snail's pace. Collecting souvenirs is prohibited," the tour guide admonishes. With less vehemence, he warns, "Coral also causes painful cuts when you touch it."

On the beach, I marvel at the pristine, white sand; swaying palm trees; and crystal-clear water. I delight as pelicans, seagulls, and tropical birds soar against the cloudless, azure sky.

Flippers and snorkel in hand, we climb into a boat. Our hair blows in the wind as the boat jets to our diving spot. At our destination, the motor abruptly halts. The sounds of silence resonate upon the open waters.

We plunge in and float on top of the bathwater-warm seas.

I am astonished every time as a tapestry of color is unveiled among the brilliance of angelfish, parrotfish, eels, and manatees. Thousands of fish swim in all directions in a sea of sapphire, gold, and scarlet. The fish form a backdrop of assorted shapes and sizes: some portly, others scrawny, some with piercing edges, others bowed. Sponges and coral create the underwater architecture.

I am absorbed in life beneath the surface.

Centering prayer is similar. You visit "the deep"—your inner sanctuary—and experience the fullness of a rich, interior life. It is a wonderful way to become centered and move deeper into relationship with God. During centering prayer, you sit in silence, enjoy God's company, and rest in His love. You move out of the mode of *doing* and striving into one of *being*.

When snorkeling, whitecaps on the surface of the water rock the boat. But the water beneath the surface is calm. Fish swim contentedly.

Centering prayer helps you journey inward, past the choppy waters of everyday life, to the tranquility within. You are freed to enjoy God's presence in calmer waters. It provides the opportunity for spiritual renewal and a peaceful time out from the noise of an external world. You move beyond thoughts, activity, and emotional turmoil into the presence of God.

This is not to imply centering prayer is the only method for experiencing God's presence, or that it should replace other types of prayer. Many wonderful books have been written about different forms of prayer. Other kinds of prayer, listening to inspirational music, reading Scripture, and walking in nature are wonderful ways to commune with God.

As you move deeper toward union with God, you begin hearing and trusting in divine guidance moment by moment. This opens your heart and helps you more closely align your will with God's.

As you enter into the fullness of the divine presence, you are emptied of some of the emotional baggage you may be experiencing. Old wounds begin to heal. It is easier to keep problems in perspective. An emotional upset may seem less significant after twenty minutes in centering prayer.

Personal Experience

Centering prayer is different from secular meditation. I began meditating almost thirty years ago and later switched to centering prayer. Secular meditation was a beneficial relaxation technique, but I never experienced the divine connectedness of centering prayer.

Centering prayer is not a relaxation technique, although relaxation is a benefit. While centered, as with all types of prayer, you enter into relationship with God.

The difference between secular meditation and centering prayer is one of resting versus resting *in God*.

Graceful Strategies

Let's consider the following strategies for centering prayer:

- Practice centering prayer.

- Experience God's presence throughout the day.

Practice centering prayer

Centering prayer is a two-stage process.

The first stage is to settle into stillness and become aware of God's presence. Quakers call this centering down. It involves coming into the present moment by quieting the mind, letting go of problems, and releasing distractions.

Find a quiet place and let family members know you do not want to be interrupted. Sit comfortably. Begin repeating a sacred phrase or word: for example, *peace, Lord, love, God is love.* This helps you quiet internal dialogue and become more God-centered. Repeat your sacred phrase effortlessly, in silence, until you reach a state of stillness. Do not concentrate or work at it, just gently repeat it.

Some feel the sacred phrase should be a one-syllable word. Others prefer a longer word or short phrase. Some suggest using the same sacred phrase all the time. Others alter it. Some people prefer to visualize an image instead of repeating a phrase. Experiment and see what works for you.

The intent is to move away from thoughts and into the presence of God.

The second stage of centering prayer is sitting in silence in the presence of God. This is a time for you to listen, not talk, to God. If you are struggling with a problem, gently ask for guidance. Then listen for the response.

If your mind wanders, effortlessly return to your sacred phrase until you reach a state of stillness. As you sit in silence, you can still hear the phone ring and the house creak. Thoughts will come and go, especially during times of stress. Do not fight them or struggle to make your mind go blank. If a distracting thought is persistent, write it down on a notepad to release it, or think of a visual image such as a river to carry it away.

For some people, the effect of centering prayer is dramatic from the start. Others find sitting quietly difficult at first. A friend claimed it was the longest five minutes of her life when she tried it. You will become more comfortable sitting in stillness the more you practice. As you move deeper into the presence of God, you will find the deep silence is full and rich.

It helps to choose a regular time so it becomes part of your daily routine. Twenty minutes twice a day—once in the morning before you start your day and again in late afternoon to carry you through the rest of the evening—is the guidance I received. Experiment to see what works for you. Some people prefer a longer session in the morning. If you find these timelines to be impossible, do what works. Any amount of time is better than none.

If possible, choose a regular place for prayer: among the pillows on your bed, in the corner of an unused room, on a chair in the family room.

The time and place should be quiet and free of interruptions. Some get up early before others awaken. Some wait until after the children go to school. A friend places a sign on the door to let her husband know it is her quiet time and she does not want to be disturbed.

Experience God's presence throughout the day

Centering prayers said during your regular prayer time are maintenance prayers.

For a deeper relationship with God, centering prayers can also be said throughout the day, not just during a regular quiet time. The Apostle Paul said to "pray continually."[115]

You can experience God's presence by silently repeating a sacred phrase as you go about your daily routine. This helps you experience peace and brings you back to center amid external noise and chaos. You can do this anytime, anywhere:

for example, while driving, waiting in line, doing chores around the house, or during a meeting at work. Of course, other forms of prayer and reading Scripture are also wonderful ways to experience God's presence.

Another form of centering prayer is the emergency fix. The emergency fix is a quick form of centering prayer said during times of crises and emotional upsets—instead of counting to ten to calm you down. You can silently repeat a short, sacred phrase or passage of Scripture anytime you are emotionally upset. This helps turn potentially tumultuous experiences into spiritual occasions. Emergency fixes can be said throughout the day to bring you back to center and transform a situation of disunity into one of harmony.

Gratitude and Grace

The following is an entry from my gratitude journal. It shocks me to this day. "I am thankful for the drink of cold water from the water fountain in the Anchorage, Alaska, airport."

I had just been halfway around the world on an incredible two-week vacation to China. Four tour guides—two from the United States and two from China—pampered our group of twelve tourists.

My memorable journal entry? Was it Tiananmen Square? No. The Great Wall? No. The Giant Panda Reserve? I am privileged for these experiences. And my Chinese friends were wonderful. But my journal entry is one of gratitude for a drink of water. After drinking bottled water for two weeks, a spontaneous drink from the water fountain was a delight.

My journal entry below it reads, "It was a blessing to have my family welcome us home. I am thankful Mom, Dad, [my brother] Campy, Dave, Erin, and I stayed up talking until 3:30 A.M., and Erin and I until 5:00 A.M. Family is such a wonderful blessing."

I keep a gratitude journal as suggested by Sarah Ban Breathnach in *Simple Abundance*. From the first entry I penned, it was evident joy is not found through money and material things. A drink of water. A loving family. I felt like Dorothy who went all the way to the Oz before realizing what she wanted was in her own backyard.

As the Wall Fell

I once read children want more, not because they don't have enough, but because they have too much. While traveling through Germany, a young woman who grew up under communist rule in East Germany confirmed this theory. I asked her to compare life in Germany before and after the Berlin wall came down. I puffed up, expecting her to gush about the virtues of the west and our wonderful country.

Her reply surprised me. Yes, she was happy to live in a free society. But now that people have more, they want more, she explained. Girls who were happy with one doll are now dissatisfied with three because their friend has five. Grownups once content with a modest home strive for a bigger one. Her parents preferred life when the price of a loaf of bread was the same in every store in the country. Now they shop for bargains. She summarized the difference: as the wall tumbled, envy and ingratitude rose.

William Penn, a Quaker and one of the founders of Pennsylvania, called envy "the greatest of monsters as well as the root of all evil." The Buddha described envy as "blind craving or desire" and the root of our suffering.[116]

A group of people who won the lottery participated in a study of the effects of winning on happiness five years later. The results indicated the lottery had no effect on happiness. People who were happy before winning were happy after. Unhappy people were still unhappy.

In a Nazi concentration camp, one man asked another how he could kneel and give thanks to God. The man replied, "I told God I am thankful I am not like them."[117]

Mind/body medicine physicians have observed patients who are grateful heal faster, are happier, and have an easier time making positive changes. Gratitude can positively affect your body chemistry and improve your body's resistance to disease.[118] A study on the effects of optimism on health reported heart patients weathered surgery better when they remained optimistic.[119]

Gratitude is the result of internal condition, not external circumstance. It is accepting what is instead of dwelling on what is not.

What keeps us from being grateful?

- Insisting things happen our way instead of trusting God's plan.

- Disconnecting the gift from the Giver.

Graceful Strategies

Let's consider the following strategies for living in gratitude and grace:

- Bask in graceful surroundings.

- Trust God's plan.

- Observe the hand of God.

Bask in graceful surroundings

Hundreds of children lined the edge of a field dotted in purple, yellow, and pink for the annual community Easter egg hunt. Baskets in hand, one foot in front of the other, the children postured themselves for a quick start. Among the crowd of three-foot-tall participants stood our Erin.

Doting parents that we are, Dave and I coached Erin on the fine art of Easter-egg hunting. Our most astute instruction: "When they say *go,* run as fast as you can."

The whistle blew. The field of Easter became a mass of kids. They plucked eggs from the turf and placed them in their Easter baskets.

But where was Erin?

Erin was three. Both Dave and I had always kept a judicious eye on her in public. And now, in seconds, she had disappeared among the swarm of children.

We searched among the egg gatherers for our golden egg. We could not find her, but we found a friend also on the hunt for a lost child.

Praises! At last, we spotted Erin running toward us.

Erin had heeded our lesson well. When the whistle blew, she ran as fast as she could. And ran. And ran. Past all of the eggs, to the other side of the field.

She returned—with an empty basket.

The next year I took Erin to a smaller Easter egg hunt with friends. It began the same way—salivating children waiting to begin the hunt. On the word *go,* the pack took off.

History repeated itself. This year Erin had company in her sprint across the field. They raced to the far side where the grass appeared greener. And it was greener—because the grass had no eggs in it.

It was fascinating to gaze over the plethora of eggs on the near side of the field as the searchers hunted in vain on the far side. They overlooked what had surrounded them to chase after what they did not have.

When we look too far, we miss what is near.

How often has my neighbor's grass appeared greener than mine? How many times have I run over the treasures I do have in search of the ones I do not?

Can you relate?

Maybe you have some rotten eggs in your basket. Perhaps you are struggling with relationship problems, financial troubles, or health problems. Maybe you are feeling unfairly accused or under-appreciated. It's not easy being grateful when eggs rot.

Hear the hope found in Isaiah: "He tends his flock like a shepherd: He gathers the lambs in his arms and carries them close to his heart."[120] "Do not be afraid, for I am with you."[121]

Exasperated, the Easter egg hunters returned with empty baskets, only to discover what they were searching for lay by the starting line—and had been close to them at the beginning of the hunt.

God "satisfies every need there is."[122]

Return to the near side of the field. If you bask in the gifts of grace that surround you, you will be grateful. And your basket will never be empty.

Trust God's plan

Fleas. I find the idea of being thankful for fleas outrageous. But Corrie ten Boom reveals she learned to be thankful for them in her wonderful book, *The Hiding Place*.[123]

Ten Boom and her devout Christian family hid Jews from the Gestapo in their Holland home. A sting operation exposed their participation in the Dutch resistance movement. The Gestapo raided their home and confined them to concentration camps.

Fleas infested the concentration camp in Ravensbruck, Germany, where ten Boom and her sister Betsie were sent. Toilets overflowed. It reeked from the foul odor of poor plumbing and sweat. Rags hung for windows instead of glass. Stains spotted the bedding. Conditions were so cramped ten Boom felt her sister's heartbeat as they slept.

And yet, Betsie received the message "give thanks in all circumstances."[124]

Only three letters bother me about this teaching: A-L-L.

Obediently, Betsie gave thanks for their surroundings, including the fleas.

The women gathered nightly to worship and read from a Bible smuggled in by ten Boom. The prison was temporarily transformed into a sanctuary, swathed in peace.

Oddly, the guards did not enter the women's living quarters, which freed the women to worship in secret. One day the women learned why: The fleas kept the guards from entering the room!

God sent the fleas, ten Boom reasoned, so the women could escape the madness during worship.

How do we "give thanks in all circumstances"? By trusting in God's plan—even while living among fleas.

Observe the hand of God

All of our blessings are gifts of grace. Author Thomas Merton said, "To be grateful is to recognize the love of God in everything He has given us—and He has given us everything. Every breath we draw is a gift of His love."[125]

Gratitude is the fruit of becoming aware of the blessings of grace that surround you and acknowledging the source of all gifts. To be ungrateful is to disregard the Giver.

Notice the graceful beauty of a rose, trees in autumn, and a newborn baby.

Watch as your table is filled with daily bread.

Trust your future to the Planner of it.

Observe the parting of the clouds.

If you have ever flown on a stormy day, you have likely noticed the sun shining above the clouds.

The rays of grace always shine. God is always at work and always with you, even during storms.

Notice. Watch. Trust. Observe. And bear the fruit: gratitude.

Solitude

"Hurry up and eat. You can chew in the car," I told Erin when she was young. This is not my proudest moment of motherhood, but I was in a rush.

I wish I could say that is the only time I've felt pressed for time. But my heart has pounded on more than one occasion. I've written notes, talked on the phone, and checked e-mail at the same time. I've tried to listen and read the trailers at the bottom of the television screen simultaneously, although I'm not good at it. I have been filled with the Spirit, listening to inspirational music, driving to church when *honk, honk,* I signal the driver who cuts me off. How does that mood shift happen?

Our days are busy. It's tough to take time out from the daily frenzy to just *be*. Eugene Peterson, author of *The Message,* wrote, "Busyness is the enemy of spirituality. It is essentially laziness. It is doing the easy thing instead of the hard thing. It is filling our time with our own actions instead of paying attention to God's actions. It is taking charge."[126]

Aching to Seek

Loving family and friends surround me. And yet, sometimes, the dull ache of loneliness sets in. Sometimes it comes when I've been writing for a while and need to get out. But I've experienced the feelings in the middle of a crowd.

The ache, I've learned, only masquerades as pain. It is really a seeking. The urging is not for activity and crowds, but for solitude. The emptiness is a yearning for fullness that can only be experienced deep in the presence of God.

Here is the amazing thing: I have felt alone in a crowd, but I have never felt lonely in the solitude of One.

Solitary Delight

Solitude is a state of profound stillness—a thundering, inner silence. It helps you shut out the noise of an external world. This frees you to commune with God and hear His voice. You move from *doing* to *being*. It is a wonderful way to practice spiritual renewal and open your heart to the blessings of grace.

Solitude provides refuge from the madness. It helps you experience peace in the midst of chaos. Inner turmoil fades into a rich, inner fullness. It gives you a chance to take a vacation from your problems for a while. The serenity of going inward to reach your inner sanctuary is not boring or lonesome.

Graceful Strategies

Let's consider the following strategies for practicing solitude:

- Experience solitude anywhere, anytime.

- Be.

Experience solitude anywhere, anytime

Practice solitude anywhere, anytime. Solitude is an internal condition, not an external circumstance. You can experience it in the middle of a crowd and not experience it alone in the wilderness. Solitude is not synonymous with being alone, although seclusion is a wonderful way to experience it.

Capture moments throughout the day: laying in bed at night, before getting up in the morning, enjoying the flowers along a path as you enter a restaurant, walking to the car and feeling the sunshine on your back, taking a detour on a country road and appreciating its beauty.

Schedule time in your day. Several times a year, devote a larger block of time for spiritual renewal—a morning, an afternoon, a day.

Practice solitude anywhere: an empty bedroom, by a mountain stream, at the beach, on a park bench near a favorite tree in the middle of the city, in the car waiting to pick your child up from school.

Be

Solitude is a state of being; describing how to practice it is an incongruity. Nonetheless, a brief depiction is in order.

Simply, be in the presence of God. Listen and see much. Talk little. Pray. Read Scripture. Listen to inspirational music. Walk in nature. Stand in awe at the wonder of God's masterpiece. Allow yourself to be immersed in peace and grace.

CHAPTER SIX

Growing Like a Child

"Who gets the highest rank in God's kingdom?" the disciples asked Jesus.[127] In our material world, this would likely be the privileged, the accomplished, winners of awards, and those in positions of power and control.

But Jesus called a little child over and replied, "I tell you the truth, unless you change and become like little children, you will never enter the kingdom of heaven. Therefore, whoever humbles himself like this child is the greatest in the kingdom of heaven."[128]

My favorite baby picture of Erin was taken in the hospital delivery room when she was just minutes old.

I have often wondered why I love this picture. Erin is wrapped snuggly in a snow-white baby blanket. Her lips are in a pout. Her face is scrunched up and surrounded by the frills of her baby bonnet. She looks so helpless, so vulnerable, and so dependent. And as I write the final pages of this book, I now understand—these are the reasons I love this picture.

My baby in the picture could not walk, talk, read, or write. She had no money, power, or status, and had not yet earned any certificates of achievement. She could not even vote. She slept a lot and never sought control. She only wanted love. And she had the wisdom to accept every ounce of unconditional love Dave and I lavished on her.

Erin was totally dependent on us to feed her, clothe her, shelter her, and love her.

Self-sufficiency was not her way. She let us know her every need. Her soft gurgle beckoned us when she was lonely, cold, afraid, hungry, or ready to be changed. The time of day did not matter. She summoned us frequently—often in the middle of the night.

She was never too proud to seek us.

She trusted us to meet her needs.

As I have journeyed through the pages of this book, I am learning how to be more like the infant in my favorite baby picture. And since you are still with me, I suspect the same is true for you.

For as we grow in grace, we become more childlike. I hope we are growing together—humble, like a child.

May many graceful moments satisfy the longing of your heart.

Always remember this: You create loving relationships, love yourself, and live with meaning by choosing to open your heart to grace.

Grace is God's part.

Choice is yours.

Choose to open your heart to grace, moment by moment. Develop an awareness of the blessings of grace given to you. Receive the gift that is always present and always free. Everything good in life flows from God's grace.

Enter into a relationship with God. Allow God's power to work through you. Let God work His will in you. Ask Him for help. Relinquish self-sufficiency, recognize your dependence on, surrender to, and trust in God. And leave the outcome to Him.

Instead of knowing about God, know God.

Experience a transformation.

As you put down the mask and trudge through the mud, watch as the masterpiece is unveiled. I hope a renewed understanding of your worth helps you fear less and love more. Your value is a gift of grace; you are valuable because God created you. If you find yourself weary, remember to move away from "I want what I want" and trust in God to provide what you need. Turn problems into opportunities by seeking grace in the darkness.

I am confident you are becoming a moonbeam of grace and administering grace to others. I trust you are learning to rely on the power and wisdom of the Holy Spirit. I presume you are accepting other people and circumstances more, and trying to control them less.

May you live a life full of passion, purpose, and meaning by living God's plan for you. Draw on the unique talents given to you. Treasure the journey without being too anxious about the outcome.

My hope is you continue to grow—humble, like a child.

My prayer is that your life is full of meaning and that you experience relationships of grace.

On the Wings of Grace[*]

Behind my mask and mortal schemes,
Are tears and fears and broken dreams.

If I seek, will You take my hand,
And dance with me across the land?

Today I come on bended knee,
Surrender and trust in You for me.

Come rest upon my broken heart,
Transform me into Your work of art.

World of wonder, from earth to sky,
On the wings of grace, we fly.

Chris Karcher
Relationships of Grace

---

* A free print that contains this poem and accompanying
artwork is available for a limited time at
www.RelationshipsOfGrace.com

Notes

Chapter 1: Moonbeams of Grace

[1] Matthew 22:36–40.

[2] Romans 13:10 NLT.

[3] 1 John 4:7.

[4] John 5:30.

[5] As quoted in Stephen Covey, *Seven Habits of Highly Effective People* (New York, NY: Simon and Schuster, 1989), p. 319.

[6] Joyce Meyer, *Life in the Word* (ABCFM), 16 October 2002.

[7] 2 Corinthians 12:9.

[8] Gerald May, *The Awakened Heart* (New York, NY: HarperCollins Publishers, 1991), p. 7.

[9] 1 Peter 4:10.

[10] As quoted in Barbara Johnson, *Boundless Love* (Grand Rapids, MI: ZondervanPublishingHouse, 2001), pp. 162–163.

[11] Viktor E. Frankl, *Man's Search for Meaning* (New York, NY: Washington Square Press, 1984), pp. 32–33 and 86.

[12] Romans 12:1–2 MSG.

[13] Romans 12:1–2.

Chapter 2: Loving Yourself

[14] Genesis 1:27 NLT.

[15] Psalm 8:5 NLT.

[16] Ephesians 2:10 NLT.

[17] As quoted by Chuck Swindoll, *Insight for Living,* broadcast on Salt Lake City, Utah: KANN, 29 September 1999.

[18] Romans 12:1–2 NLT, emphasis mine.

[19] Display item at the *Declaration of Independence* exhibit, Utah State Capital, 20 February 2002.

[20] *The Oprah Winfrey Show,* ~1999.

[21] Romans 12:1–2 NLT, emphasis mine.

[22] A free set of worksheets in journal format is available for a limited time at www.RelationshipsOfGrace.com.

[23] Soren Kierkegaard, *The Prayers of Kierkegaard,* ed. Perry le Fevre (Chicago, IL: University of Chicago Press, 1956), p. 147, quoted in John Ortberg, *The Life You've Always Wanted* (Grand Rapids, MI: Zondervan, 1997), p. 16.

[24] Ian Grey, *Stalin* (Garden City, NY: Doubleday, 1979), p. 457, and Alex De Jonge, *Stalin and the Shaping of the Soviet Union* (New York: William Morrow, 1986), p. 450, quoted in Max Lucado, *The Applause of Heaven* (Word Publishing, 1996), p. 73.

[25] http://www.ozclub.org/storyofoz.asp, 28 February 2002, and http://www.ozclub.org/members_2001.htm, 28 February 2002.

[26] Lloyd Ogilvie, *Facing the Future Without Fear* (Ann Arbor, MI: Vine Books, 1999), p. 22, quoted in John Ortberg, *If You Want to Walk on Water You've Got to Get Out of the Boat,* (Grand Rapids, MI: ZondervanPublishingHouse, 2001), p. 118.

[27] Matthew 22:36–40.

[28] 1 Peter 5:7.

[29] Jerri Nielsen, *Ice Bound* (Miramax, 2001).

[30] Exodus 3:12.

[31] Joshua 1:9 NLT.

[32] 1 John 4:18.

[33] Psalm 149:4 MSG.

[34] Philip Yancey, *What's So Amazing About Grace?* (Grand Rapids, MI: ZondervanPublishingHouse, 1997), pp. 71 and 45.

[35] As quoted in Gerald May, *The Awakened Heart* (New York, NY: Harper Collins, 1991), p. 219.

[36] A free set of worksheets in journal format is available for a limited time at www.RelationshipsOfGrace.com.

[37] Matthew 5:43–44.

[38] 1 John 4:4b.

[39] Stedman Graham, *Good Morning America* interview, 05 September 2000.

[40] As quoted in Steven K. Scott, *Simple Steps to Impossible Dreams* (New York, NY: Simon & Schuster, 1998), p. 120.

[41] 1 Peter 4:1–2 MSG.

[42] Proverbs 3:5.

[43] Romans 8:28.

[44] Corrie ten Boom, *The Hiding Place* (Grand Rapids, MI: Chosen Books, 1984).

[45] 2 Corinthians 12:7–10.

[46] Psalm 34:18 MSG.

[47] As quoted in Louise Hay, *Gratitude: A Way of Life* (Carlsbad, CA: Hay House, 1996), p 253.

[48] Erin Kramp, *Living with the End in Mind* (New York, NY: Three Rivers Press, 1998), p. 154.

[49] Marlo Morgan, *Mutant Message Down Under* (New York, NY: HarperPerennial, 1994), pp. 51 and 93.

[50] 1 Corinthians 10:13 MSG.

[51] As quoted in Max Lucado, *He Still Moves Stones* (Word, 1993), p. 78.

[52] A free set of worksheets in journal format is available for a limited time at www.RelationshipsOfGrace.com.

[53] Genesis 3.

[54] Romans 5:3–4 teaches, "suffering produces perseverance; perseverance, character; and character, hope."

[55] Psalm 37:4.

[56] Romans 1:28–31.

[57] Joan Borysenko, *Guilt Is the Teacher, Love Is the Lesson* (New York, NY: Warner Books, 1990), p. 179.

[58] As quoted in Stephen Covey, *Seven Habits of Highly Effective People* (New York, NY: Simon and Schuster, 1989), p 72.

Chapter 3: Loving Others

[59] Deepak Chopra, *Larry King Live* interview, ~September 2000.

[60] John 14:16 AMP.

[61] Romans 8:26–27, Luke 12:12.

[62] Ezekiel 36:26–27 MSG.

[63] Galatians 5:22–23.

[64] Philippians 2:13 NLT.

[65] Proverbs 3:6 MSG.

[66] As quoted in the CLASS newsletter, 11 February 2003.

[67] A free set of worksheets in journal format is available for a limited time at www.RelationshipsOfGrace.com.

[68] John Marks Templeton, *Worldwide Laws of Life* (Radnor, PA: Templeton Foundation Press, 1997), pp. 10–11.

[69] Matthew 7:12.

[70] Galatians 6:7.

[71] As quoted in Erich Fromm, *To Have or to Be?* (Harper & Row, 1976) p. 122.

[72] Matthew 22:37–40.

[73] 1 John 4:20–21.

[74] 1 Peter 3.

[75] Deuteronomy 32:35.

[76] Deuteronomy 32:36.

[77] A free set of worksheets in journal format is available for a limited time at www.RelationshipsOfGrace.com.

Chapter 4: Living with Meaning

[78] Viktor E. Frankl, *Man's Search for Meaning* (New York, NY: Washington Square Press, 1984), pp. 126–127 and 137–138.

[79] M. Scott Peck, *The Road Less Traveled* (New York, NY: Simon & Schuster, 1978), p. 311.

[80] As quoted in *Quotemeal* from *Heartlight,* 2 March 2002.

[81] Jeff Bezos, *The Oprah Winfrey Show* interview, ~November 1999.

[82] *The Founding Fathers,* shown on the History Channel, ~May 2000.

[83] Romans 12:6.

[84] Jeremiah 29:11.

[85] Proverbs 3:5–6.

[86] Deepak Chopra, *Quantum Healing* (Bantam Books, 1989), quoted in Marianne Williamson, *A Return to Love* (New York, NY: HarperPaperbacks, 1993), p. 227.

[87] Proverbs 13:7.

[88] Erich Fromm, *To Have or to Be?* (Harper & Row, 1976) pp. 15 and 87.

[89] As quoted in Erich Fromm, *To Have or to Be?* (Harper & Row, 1976) p. 61.

[90] As quoted on *The Oprah Winfrey Show,* June 2002.

[91] Lance Armstrong, *Today Show* interview, 29 July 2002.

[92] As told on *The Opray Winfrey Show.*

[93] http://www.oprah.com/about/press/about_press_bio.jhtml, rev. May 2002, 3 August 2002.

[94] Gerald May, *Addiction and Grace* (New York, NY: HarperCollins, 1988) p. 154.

[95] John 3:8.

[96] As quoted in Philip Yancey, *What's So Amazing About Grace?* (Grand Rapids, MI: Zondervan, 1997), p. 245.

[97] John 13:5.

[98] Mother Teresa, *The Joy in Living* (New York, NY: Penguin, 1996), p. 372.

[99] As quoted in Max Lucado, *He Still Moves Stones* (Word, 1993), p. 70.

Chapter 5: The Spiritual Journey

[100] A free set of worksheets in journal format is available for a limited time at www.RelationshipsOfGrace.com.

[101] Psalm 51:10 AMP.

[102] Proverbs 4:23.

[103] Romans 12:1–2 MSG.

[104] 2 Corinthians 3:3.

[105] Deuteronomy 6:5.

[106] Deuteronomy 10:13.

[107] As quoted in Steve McVey, *Grace Land* (Eugene, OR: Harvest House, 2001), p. 137.

[108] Luke 17:21.

[109] 1 John 4:4.

[110] Jeremiah 29:13–14.

[111] Matthew 7:7.

[112] As quoted in Timothy Jones, *The Art of Prayer* (New York, NY: Ballantine Books, 1997), p. 133, quoted in Max Lucado, *Just Like Jesus* (Word Publishing, 1998), p. 71.

[113] For additional information on centering prayer, refer to Thomas Keating, *Open Mind Open Heart* (New York, NY: Continuum Publishing, 2001); M. Basil Pennington, *Centered Living* (Liguori, MI: Liguori/Triumph, 1999); Contemplative Outreach, Ltd. national office, 9 William Street, P.O. Box 737, Butler, NJ 07405, Tel.: 201-838-3384.

[114] William McGill as quoted in *Quotemeal* from *Heartlight*, 9 August 2002.

[115] 1 Thessalonians 5:17.

[116] *The Encyclopedia of Religious Quotations,* ed. Frank Mead (Westwood, NJ: Fleming Revell, 1965) and *The Encyclopedia of Eastern Philosophy and Religion* (Boston, MA: Shambhala, 1989), p. 96, quoted in Leonard Felder, *The Ten Challenges* (New York, NY: Three Rivers Press, 1997), p. 206.

[117] As quoted on *West Wing,* 3 October 2001.

[118] Louise Hay, *Gratitude: A Way of Life* (Carlsbad, CA: Hay House, 1996), pp. 174, 175, 177, and 178.

[119] *Good Morning America*, September 1999.

[120] Isaiah 40:11.

[121] Isaiah 43: 5.

[122] Acts 17:25 NLT.

[123] Corrie ten Boom, *The Hiding Place* (Grand Rapids, MI: Chosen Books, 1984), pp. 180–187.

[124] 1 Thessalonians 5:18.

[125] Thomas Merton as quoted in *Quotemeal* from *Heartlight,* 15 October 2001.

[126] As quoted in *The Door,* November/December 1991.

Chapter 6: Growing Like a Child

[127] Matthew 18:1 MSG.

[128] Matthew 18:2–4.

Chris Karcher has enjoyed a distinguished career as author, professional speaker, and manager of multimillion-dollar programs while working in industry.

Chris is the author of three books, ten technical documents, and two adult Sunday school curriculums. Her books include *Amazing Things I Know About You,* the *Relationships of Grace Workbook,* and *Relationships of Grace.* She is currently writing her next book *Relationships of Grace Miracles.* Chris teaches adult Sunday school. She is the author of class curriculums *Creating Loving Relationships: Loving God, Others, and Self* and *Majestic Grace* and coauthor of *Christianity 101.* Chris served on the Board of Directors for the National Speakers Association Utah chapter.

Chris has been married to her husband, Dave, for twenty-five years. They have a wonderful daughter, Erin.

For information about *Relationships of Grace* speeches, seminars, and products, or to join our mailing list, please contact:

www.RelationshipsOfGrace.com
news@RelationshipsOfGrace.com
Fax: 801-547-0928
Relationships of Grace, P.O. Box 1043, Layton, Utah 84041-1043

Share Your Story in Our Next Book

You are invited to submit a story, anecdote, or quotation for possible inclusion in our next book. This may be your own original material or something you have read that was written by someone else. Both the author and contributor will be acknowledged. A seventy-five-word biography of the author will be included. Multiple submissions are welcome.

For *Relationships of Grace Miracles*, two types of stories are needed. First, stories about gifts of grace—miracles, twists of fate, everyday blessings, and divine incidents disguised as ordinary events and coincidences. Second, stories for each section in the table of contents at the front of this book (e.g., The Naked Choice, Loving Yourself, From Fear to Love, etc.). Please indicate the applicable section with your submission. If your story fits into more than one section, write the story once with a brief explanation of how the story could be adapted to multiple sections.

Stories should encourage and inspire readers through emotion or humor. Suggested length is 350 to 1500 words. Please use stories, illustrations, and metaphors to teach. Avoid preaching and religious jargon. Stories should reach across denominational boundaries.

For complete guidelines and the submission deadline, please visit our website, send a fax or email, or mail your request with a stamped, self-addressed envelope to:

Relationships of Grace
P.O. Box 1043
Layton, Utah 84041-1043
Fax: 801-547-0928
www.RelationshipsOfGrace.com
guidelines@relationshipsofgrace.com

You will only hear from us if your story is selected. Due to time constraints, submissions will not be returned.

The preferred method to submit a story is a Word or Word Perfect file sent as an attachment via email to:
miracles@RelationshipsOfGrace.com
Or, you may fax or mail a hardcopy as indicated above.

Free Offers[*]

Visit www.RelationshipsOfGrace.com for the following free resources:

- A set of worksheets in journal format containing selected self-reflective questions from *Relationships of Grace* and *Relationships of Grace Workbook*

- A print and accompanying artwork of the poem *On the Wings of Grace*

- The *Relationships of Grace* newsletter

Inspirational Resources by Chris Karcher

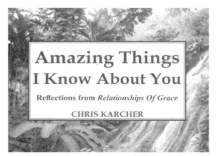

ISBN 1-932356-52-5

Amazing Things I Know About You

You are amazing. Discover the real reason you are of value; learn how to unveil the masterpiece within through these reflections from *Relationships of Grace*. Whether for your own personal enrichment or as a gift for a friend, *Amazing Things I Know About You* shares inspirational messages of encouragement and hope.

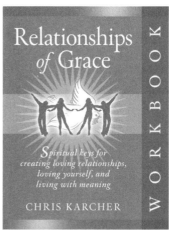

ISBN 1-932356-53-3

Relationships of Grace Workbook

Experience true change from the inside out as you journey deeper through this unique workbook. Reflect on thought-provoking questions, chronicle lessons learned, and journal personal insights. This is a terrific resource for Sunday school classes, book clubs, Bible studies, small groups, and personal growth.

**Available from selected bookstores, or
Call 1-877-GET-GRACE (1-877-438-4722), or
Visit www.relationshipsofgrace.com**

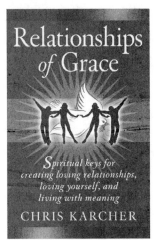

Relationships
of Grace

*Spiritual keys for
creating loving relationships,
loving yourself, and
living with meaning*

CHRIS KARCHER

CD, abridged
ISBN 1-932356-20-7
Audiocassette, abridged
ISBN 1-932356-21-5

*Relationships of Grace
Audio Books*
Listen to delightful stories
with powerful messages on
CD and audiocassette. You
will be entertained and
uplifted as you learn the
spiritual keys for creating
loving relationships, loving
yourself, and living with
meaning.